The Radicality of Love

Theory Redux

Series editor: Laurent de Sutter

Published Titles
Roberto Esposito, *Persons and Things*
Srećko Horvat, *The Radicality of Love*
Dominic Pettman, *Infinite Distraction*

The Radicality of Love

Srećko Horvat

polity

Copyright © Srećko Horvat 2016

The right of Srećko Horvat to be identified as Author of this Work has been asserted in accordance with the UK Copyright, Designs and Patents Act 1988.

First published in 2016 by Polity Press

Polity Press
65 Bridge Street
Cambridge CB2 1UR, UK

Polity Press
350 Main Street
Malden, MA 02148, USA

ISBN-13: 978-0-7456-9114-5
ISBN-13: 978-0-7456-9115-2(pb)

A catalogue record for this book is available from the British Library.

Library of Congress Cataloging-in-Publication Data

Horvat, Srecko.
The radicality of love / Srecko Horvat.
pages cm
Includes bibliographical references.
ISBN 978-0-7456-9114-5 (hardback) -- ISBN 978-0-7456-9115-2 (pbk.)
1. Communism and love. 2. Communism and sex. 3. Love--Political aspects.
4. Radicalism. 5. Revolutions. I. Title.
HX550.L73H67 2015
128'.46--dc23
2015014785

Typeset in 12.5 on 15 pt Adobe Garamond by
Servis Filmsetting Ltd, Stockport, Cheshire
Printed and bound in the UK by Clays Ltd, St Ives plc

The publisher has used its best endeavours to ensure that the URLs for external websites referred to in this book are correct and active at the time of going to press. However, the publisher has no responsibility for the websites and can make no guarantee that a site will remain live or that the content is or will remain appropriate.

Every effort has been made to trace all copyright holders, but if any have been inadvertently overlooked the publisher will be pleased to include any necessary credits in any subsequent reprint or edition.

For further information on Polity, visit our website:
politybooks.com

Contents

Meet me in Taksim tonight
a drink and a kiss
what in the world could be more civilized?
　Chinawoman, "Kiss in Taksim Square" (2013)

Foreplay: To Fall in Love, or Revolution

Each attempt to speak or even write about love is inevitably linked to a profound difficulty, to an anxiety: words are always insufficient. However, even if our attempt resembles a jump into dark water, we should dare to talk about love, with all the risks involved. We should try again, fail again, fail better. The necessity for this book is to be found in the following consideration: that the lover's discourse is still, like 40 years ago when Roland Barthes famously uttered this credo in his *Fragments of a Lover's Discourse*, of an extreme solitude.

It shouldn't surprise us so much that love is missing in the hypersexualized universe of the West, but what is striking is that it has no real place (does love have a place at all, or is it always already an *a-topos*?) or important role in recent upheavals all around the world, from Tahrir Square to Taksim, from Zuccotti Park to Puerta del Sol, from Hong Kong to Sarajevo. The question of love is surprisingly missing. It is hidden in the margins, whispered in tents, performed in a dark corner of the street. There are, of course, kisses on Taksim Square and passionate affairs in Zuccotti Park, but love is not the issue of serious debate. This book – sadly aware that it is only a small step in a long journey in front of us; that it is maybe only a foreplay – has to be seen as a risky contribution to this missing topic.

This attempt towards the possible meaning of radicality of love doesn't understand love in the vulgar materialistic sense of, let's say, the hippie explosion, or the "sexual revolution" of '68 that was, unfortunately, in the end primarily reduced to commodified desire, or the postmodern permissiveness where "anything goes!" It goes, or at least tries to reach, much beyond it, embarking from the following dock: it is not only enough to be true to your desire and ready to follow it until the end – Lacan's famous dictum: *ne pas céder sur son desir* ("Do not give up on your desire"); what

2

is needed is a Duty to reinvent it from the very beginning each time over. Rimbaud's famous credo that "love has to be reinvented" is the best recapitulation of this revolutionary duty.

It is wonderfully captured in one of the most beautiful instances of the fight against habit ever conducted, in Kierkegaard's *Works of Love*:

> Let the thunder of a hundred cannon remind you three times daily to resist the force of habit. Like that powerful Eastern emperor, keep a slave who reminds you daily – keep hundreds. Have a friend who reminds you every time he sees you. Have a wife who, in love, reminds you early and late – but be careful that all this also does not become a habit! For you can become accustomed to hearing the thunder of a hundred cannon so that you can sit at the table and hear the most trivial, insignificant things far more clearly than the thunder of the hundred cannon – which you have become accustomed to hearing. And you can become so accustomed to having a hundred slaves remind you every day that you no longer hear, because through habit you have acquired the ear which hears and still does not hear.[1]

The worst thing that can happen to love is habit. Love is – if it is really love – a form of eternal dynamism and at the same time fidelity to the first encounter. It is a tension, or better, a sort of dialectics: between dynamism (this constant re-invention) and fidelity (to this fatal and unexpected *crack in the world*). The same holds for Revolution. The moment when a revolution stops to reinvent, not only social and human relations, but stops reinventing its own presuppositions, we usually end up in a *re-action*, in a regression.

A truly revolutionary moment is like love; it is a crack in the world, in the usual running of things, in the dust that is layered all over in order to prevent anything New. It is a moment when air becomes thick and at the same time you can breathe more than ever. But remember Kierkegaard: when you get accustomed to hearing the thunder of a hundred cannon so that you can sit oblivious at the table, you know the revolution is at stake and the moment of counter-revolution lurks behind the thunder. The moment when you get used to the thunder of the hundred cannon, the truth of the event disappears. This is the reason why all these superficial classifications

("Arab Spring," "Occupy Movement," "New Left," etc.), which evolved from the eternal drive of people to alienate things by definitions, are dangerously misleading and become untrue to the original event, or: a desire (not from the past, but) from the future.

There is no such thing as the Arab Spring. There is no such thing as the Occupy Movement. Yes, they all share inherent characteristics (from the form of organization to most of the goals), and we are currently witnessing a specific political sequence that might bring tremendous changes (or end up in a total fiasco), but to identify them, to reduce them to the same denominator, always carries the danger of falling into the trap of simplification: to define is to limit (it is a *limes*), by definition. Of course, all these events are connected in a deeper sense. But each of this events, as much as they are part of the same sequence or pattern, carries something New.

To perceive this New, one can't say Syntagma or Puerta del Sol are the same. There is, as said, a pattern. There is, of course, a very specific historical context (from the upheavals of 2011 to the new left parties such as Syriza or Podemos) in which such revolutionary potentials occur.

But what connects them, more than anything, is something that can't be reduced to pure facts. What can't be reduced is this feeling of presence beyond classification or definitions; a presence of submergence; the feeling that you are completely alone but not abandoned, that you are more alone and unique than ever before, but more connected with a multitude than ever as well, in the very same moment. And this feeling can be described as Love. Revolution is love if it wants to be worthy of its name.

Just take the miracle that happened at Tahrir Square when Christians had put their own lives at risk protecting Muslims praying amid violence between protesters and Mubarak's supporters. They formed a "human chain" around those praying to protect them. This was – and still is – one of the most remarkable scenes from the so-called "Arab Spring"; this moment of unity, courage and … *discipline*. Wasn't that mad in the eyes of the regime? But, at the same time, wasn't that pure reason in the middle of madness? Or as Hegel would say it *à propos* Napoleon, wasn't that the "world spirit on horseback," the Godot we were waiting for in our dark times?

Something similar happened during the Iranian

Revolution. When Khomeini in March 1979 ordered women to wear the *chador*, hundreds of feminists started to gather in the courtyard of Tehran University and during the following five days of demonstrations tens of thousands protested against the veil. Then a Tahrir-like event happened: the women were surrounded by the newly formed "Party of God" (Hezbollah) and, in order to protect them, men – friends, lovers, brothers – made a circle around them.

This is a *sign* of love. And, again, it is Kierkegaard who still provides us with the best explanation of this event: one must believe in love, otherwise one will never become aware that it exists. The same goes for revolution. But why a *sign*? Because it is still not love. It is *solidarity*. Every act of solidarity contains love, it is a sort of love, but love can't be reduced to solidarity. Take charity as opposed to solidarity. Usually it contains some sort of distance: if you, for instance, come across a beggar and give him a dollar or bread, this is not yet solidarity. Even if you organize a huge charity campaign, open an account for donations, etc., this is not yet solidarity. Solidarity is something much more than mercy: usually when you appease your conscience (donate money to starving children in Africa, to use the usual Starbucks example), you can go on with your daily life as if nothing really happened. However, once you are enacting solidarity you can even abstain from charity or mercy: even if you don't give a dollar to every beggar, you can't go on with your daily life as if nothing really happened. Why? Because you carry him in your life; you live with him not like with some "integrated reject" (as we live with immigrants or refugees today), but he is a part and even a presupposition for your very action: he can never be fully integrated, because injustice can't be integrated in acts of love. This is why solidarity already contains love. In this respect, forming protective human rings around Muslims, Jews or women is a beautiful instance of solidarity, but to arrive at love one must go a step further. To love would mean to do it even when there is no event, no special occasion, or level of consciousness. That would be the true event: when love is not (only) provoked by extraordinary cracks in the world, but can be found in the seemingly boring daily activities, even repetitions, or – reinventions.

Although our present historical deadlock, with all the "autumns" that came after "springs," is

darker than ever, it is the fidelity to this possible future (Muslims and Christians fighting
together in Egypt, women and men in Iran, etc.)
that defines the true revolutionary commitment.
The time always comes when the shining path
becomes covered with dust, when enthusiasm
turns into the worst sort of depression (or what
Walter Benjamin would call "left-wing melancholy"), when a counterrevolution swallows the
last emancipatory potentials of a revolutionary
moment, but the biggest defeat would be to sink
into this: not to be defeated by the brutal reality after another defeat, but to be defeated by
the abandonment of the utopian desire. Here we
should paraphrase Mao, who in his famous quote
says that a revolution is not a dinner party, or
writing an essay, or painting a picture, but an
insurrection and act of violence by which one
class overthrows another. Today we should say
the following: Revolution is not a one-night
stand, nor is it a flirt. These are the easiest things
to do. If you perceive revolution like that you
might easily find yourself waking up after crazy
sex the next morning just to find a foreign body
in your bed. Yesterday it was the most beautiful and sensual lover, now it is just a (fucked)

body, like all those bodies left behind by the *Nymphomaniac*.

True love is much more violent than that. You can forget the foreign body, you can get over it, have another one-night stand or passionate affair, but you can never forget a real encounter, because it is an act of violence. Remember Laura from the classic 1945 Hollywood melodrama *Brief Encounter* (directed by David Lean), who in her imaginary confession to her husband, after her brief romance with a stranger at the railway station, says: "But, oh, Fred, I've been so foolish. I've fallen in love. I'm an ordinary woman. I didn't think such violent things could happen to ordinary people." She stayed with her husband, but the "brief encounter" changed the very presuppositions of her existence. Yes, love can happen even to ordinary people.

And didn't the same happen with Tahrir or Occupy Wall Street? We could, of course, say that everything had to change so that everything could stay the same (Muslim Brotherhood and the army regime in Egypt after Mubarak; Obama after Obama again, etc.), but some coordinates did change. The most difficult task is – unlike Laura, instead of returning to her husband for a variety of reasons (guilt trip, understanding, habit, the possibility of loving two at the same time, etc.) – to *endure*. Firstly, not to be deceived by a false encounter (go for the stranger at the railway station only to end up in a superficial one-night stand), and secondly, grab the chance when the real encounter appears out of nowhere and do whatever it takes (go for the stranger...). Sing if you feel like singing in front of the skyscrapers of Wall Street, protect your fellow Muslims even if bullets might start flying.

This is the true meaning of "falling in love." We take the risk, whatever the consequences might be. Even if we are aware that this fatal encounter will change the very coordinates of our daily lives, we insist on it precisely because of that. What else is there to be done?

But instead of this necessary risk of "falling in love," what we have today is a worldwide movement directed against any sort of risk: from our decadent Western permissive societies to the Islamic fundamentalists, all of them are united in the fight against desire. Even if they proclaim desire, like our Western new social inventions (Grindr, Tinder, etc.), or they prohibit desire, like the fundamentalists of ISIS or Iran, they are aiming at abolishing chance, the very moment when you really fall into something, when you are lost . . . but you still know your way better than ever.

It was Alain Badiou who in his wonderful *In Praise of Love* described the fear of "falling in love." He was struck by posters all around Paris for the Meetic internet dating site, whose ads contained slogans such as "Get love without chance!," "Be in love without falling in love," or "Get perfect love without suffering." For Badiou, this is similar to the US army propaganda of promoting the idea of "smart" bombs and "zero dead" war. Why? Because there is no war and no love without risks. A "zero risk" love is not love: if a dating service has selected your partner according to your tastes, horoscope sign, job, interests, intellect, body, etc., no chance encounters. But *falling in love* consists precisely in this contingency, in the *fall* itself.

It was Ibn Arabi, one of the most influential, but still controversial, Sufis who already understood that it is the *fall* that matters in "falling in love." Ibn Arabi understood "falling of love" as something he calls *hawa*. He classifies the concept of love in four stages. These are: *hawa, hubb, ishq,* and *wudd.*[2] The first stage of love is called *hawa*. Literally *hawa* means to fall, i.e. the falling of love or any kind of passion into the heart. A man falls in love for three reasons: 1, seeing; 2, hearing; and 3, bounties received from the Beloved. The strongest cause of *hawa* is seeing, since this does not change upon meeting the Beloved. On the other hand, the second and third causes of the *hawa* are not perfect, because love caused by hearing changes by seeing, and love caused by beneficence can cease or weaken with the ceasing of the bounties.

The object of *hawa* might be many things, and not necessarily God. Therefore, in the Qur'an God commands the believers not to follow *hawa*. *Hawa* is a kind of love for God polluted with associating partners with the love of God. It is therefore not a pure love of God.

Knowing that Allah commands His servants to purify their *hawa* and direct it to God, Ibn Arabi admits that it is impossible to eradicate *hawa* from the heart, since it is nothing but a natural sentiment. All human beings have *hawa* for a different beloved. Allah commands His servants to direct this *hawa* to Him. But in spite of God's prohibition on following *hawa*, it is impossible to eradicate its existence.

Ibn Arabi believes that non-believers possess this kind of love, because their love for God is mixed in with their love of their partners. It is no wonder that the next stage of love is something the sufis call *hubb*. It is the purification of *hawa*, and it is realized by eliminating other lovers and directing it only to God. In this sense, *hubb* is a pure and unpolluted love for God cleansed from all kinds of spiritual dirt. Ibn Arabi justifies this meaning of *hubb* from its etymology: in Arabic, a water pot is called *hubb* since water rests in it and its dirt sinks to the bottom. In this way the water becomes purified from dirt.

But there is also an excessive form of *hubb*. It is called *'ishq*. When *hubb* pervades all the body and blinds the lover's eyes except to the Beloved and circulates in the veins like blood, it is called *'ishq*. It would be something Roland Barthes described in his *Fragments of a Lover's Discourse*. If anything, Barthes' book is not about love so much as about *falling in love*. And one of the most important characteristics of falling in love is the existence of *signs*. Barthes succeeded in showing how falling in love is *a priori* a semiotic system: the lover is a natural semiotician, he sees signs everywhere and in everything. This is *'ishq*.

But still, if Barthes' "fragments" of a "lover's discourse" are mainly a journey through the signs of falling in love, what would then be *more*, something that is closer to love as such? What is for Ibn Arabi the fourth stage? It is *wudd*, an attribute general to the three above-mentioned stages of love. It is the permanency of *hubb*, *'ishq*, or *hawa* in the heart of the lover. And it is here that we enter Sufism at its best: "for the true mystic all love is divine, and the division between profane and divine love is only a surface phenomenon. If men love women because of the divine manifestation in her, this love becomes divine love, while those who love them only out of natural lusts are ignorant of the reality of creation."[3]

Take sex: if it is being done between two people who are not only attracted to one another but have fallen in love, isn't this sex the most wonderful merging of divine and profane? All those bodily fluids that are normally considered disgusting suddenly become divine. Isn't this also the level of revolution we should achieve today; wasn't the moment of Christians protecting Muslims or men protecting women during the Iranian Revolution an encounter of the divine and profane, a manifestation of *wudd*?

This brings us to one possible proposition about love: to truly know love means to come to the level of universality. There were moments when the Iranian Revolution and Tahrir Square not only overlapped, but they had the same *structure*. What might look like a discontinuity at first glance is actually a continuity. And precisely in this continuity can we find traces of universality.

This is the lesson of the beautiful example from C. L. R. James' *The Black Jacobins*: when Napoleon sent French soldiers to suppress the rebellion of slaves in Haiti, at night they heard the blacks in the forest singing the *Marseillaise* and *Ça Ira*, the emblematic songs of the French Revolution. They were, of course, shocked. They looked at the officers as if to say, "Have our barbarous enemies justice on their side? Are we no longer the soldiers of Republican France? And have we become the crude instruments of policy?"[4]

The protagonists of the Haiti Revolution took more literally *Liberté, égalité, fraternité* than the French themselves. For them it was nothing abstract, it was an anti-colonial struggle. What happened, then, resembles both the events from the Iranian Revolution and Tahrir Square. A regiment of Poles, who remembered their own struggle for emancipation, refused to join in the massacre of 600 Haitian slaves. And this is what *Liberté, égalité, fraternité* really means!

To understand the potential of this radical universality it seems we must conduct the structuralist experiment again: to understand all the revolutionary sequences on the synchrony and diachrony levels. Each part of the revolutionary history and present exists at the same time (Occupy, Syntagma, Tahrir, Taksim), and at the same time exists separated by time (Paris Commune, Haiti Revolution, October Revolution, etc.). But the true task is not only to decipher the revolutionary history on these two levels, but to detect their dialectical relation, the interaction of both, synchrony and diachrony. Take, again, the event at Tahrir Square (Christians defending Muslims) and the event from the Iranian Revolution (men defending women): at the diachronical level we can say one happened before the other, but on the synchronic level we see they are *in presentia*: it is as if they exist at the same time. Only, as it were, by transferring their diachronical relation to the synchronic level can we arrive at their true universality. In other words, we could imagine something we might call "the structuralism of resistance."

It is not only that the Haitian *Marseillaise* carries the real *pathos* of the true radicality of the French Revolution, its universal, emancipatory character, but it is at the same time as if we could hear this echo in the events of the Iranian Revolution or Tahrir Square as well. And wasn't the Tahrir Square event repeated on January 21, 2015, when more than 1,000 Muslims formed a human shield around Oslo's synagogue, offering a symbolic protection for the city's Jewish community and condemning an attack on a synagogue in neighboring Denmark. It doesn't matter whether one is Jew, Muslim, or Christian, this is the only true universality. St. Paul's *Epistles*: "There is neither Jew nor Gentile, neither slave nor free, nor is there male and female. . ."

The only one who to this day came close to such an – almost structuralist – understanding of the revolutionary universality was Peter Weiss, in his *Die Ästhetik des Widerstands*, the historical novel which was so much more than a historical novel. What Weiss did is not only a novelistic experiment that can't be categorized (isn't this the best definition of a true art work?), but even more: he conducted a *tour de force* in showing how the synchrony and diachrony of resistance can function in reality. The central thesis of *The Aesthetics of Resistance* is that precisely through this endeavor can we arrive at resistance; through education and self-education, through a constant examination of art, through a process of identification, we already commit an act of resistance. Instead of Lacan's "Subject supposed to know" (*sujet supposé savoir*) we need Rancière's "Ignorant Schoolmaster." Only by posing seemingly naive questions (for example, let's imagine the Haitian slaves asking their French colonizers: "What does *Liberté, égalité, fraternité* really mean?") can we arrive at truly radical answers.

Our journey through a possible meaning of the *Radicality of Love* must conduct an experiment of posing seemingly naive questions similar to the ones Pier Paolo Pasolini asked in 1963 when he took a 16mm camera and a microphone to travel throughout Italy, from the industrialized North to the archaic South, and questioned all sorts of people about seemingly naive topics. The result was *Comizi d'amore* (Love Meetings), a unique *cinéma vérité* documentary in which children answer how children come into the world, soldiers whether they would rather be a "Don Juan or a good dad?," football players about sexual repression, female factory workers on prostitution, virginity, homosexuality, divorce, etc.

This book is trying to explore what would happen if we were to take the microphone into our hands and if we were to, without any fear of the possible responses, stroll through the revolutionary history of the twentieth century and ask the main protagonists – from Lenin to Che Guevara, from Alexandra Kollontai to Ulrike Meinhof, from market fundamentalists to Islamic fundamentalists – seemingly naive questions on love, sex, and revolution. Moreover, it can also be understood as a modest contribution to the current upheavals all around the world – from "springs" to "occupations" – in which the question of love is surprisingly missing. It is as if, from the "Arab Spring" to the "Occupy Movement," from São Paulo to Hong Kong, from Athens to Sarajevo, there is no consciousness that we can never really imagine a different and better world without the reinvention of love. The reinvention of the world without the reinvention of love is not a reinvention at all. And this is the reason why all important revolutions of the twentieth century – from the October Revolution to the

Iranian Revolution – aimed at regulating the most intimate spheres of human life.

There is a wonderful anecdote about the Russian revolutionary Alexander Kaun that brings us, without unnecessary introductions, instantly into the topic of this book. "In Moscow," said Kaun, "when we used to attend a party, the hostess, a beautiful woman, would appear completely nude except for a pair of gold slippers. This was a test of our dedication to the Revolution. Our souls were too filled with the dream of Russian freedom to respond to a naked woman." However, many years later, it is the same revolutionary who gave a dialectical twist to his own commitment: "But now I have forgotten all the revolutionary speeches that were made at those parties. I remember only her breasts – two heavenly pillows."[5]

C'est la vie! Is it so difficult to imagine a similar conclusion of a protester from Zuccotti Park who has now grown old after all the enthusiasm he felt protesting in 2011 against the skyscrapers of Wall Street or even a protester from the Iranian Revolution of 1979: "Our souls were too filled with the dream of changing the world, but now I remember only two heavenly pillows?" Doesn't it sound like another version of the famous phrase on the front of T-shirts: "My brother went to Istanbul, and all I got was this lousy T-shirt"? Or in this context: "We believed we were making a revolution, and all I got was a memory of her breasts."

The way out of this fatal deadlock maybe lies in overcoming this binary opposition. The real question today is the following one: do we really have to choose, and is it the only choice we can make, the choice between our dedication to the Revolution or "two heavenly pillows"? What our short *Comizi d'amore* will try to propose is that the answer to the question "love *or* revolution" should be as simple and difficult (at the same time) as: love *and* revolution. Only here are we able to find the true Radicality of Love.

I

Love in the Age of Cold Intimacies

"Love has to be reinvented, that's certain."
When Arthur Rimbaud uttered these prophetic
words in his *Une Saison en Enfer* (1873), he was
criticizing the longing for security and classical
relationships.

He himself was dreaming about crusades,
unrecorded voyages of discovery, moral revolutions, and enchantment. And he even reached it
in his short and wild affair – accompanied by lots
of heavy drinking, absinthe and hashish – with
Verlaine. As we know, the older poet abandoned
his wife and infant son. In the end he fired two
shots at Rimbaud.

Although today we can only speculate whether
disappointment in love was the reason for

Rimbaud's radical escape from poetry to Africa, one thing is certain: after the urge to reinvent love, Rimbaud ended up reinventing himself. First he joined the Dutch Colonial Army in Java and soon deserted; then he went to Cyprus to work as a construction worker; in the end, he spent the rest of his life in Yemen and Ethiopia as an explorer, photographer, and even an arms dealer.

As we can see from his letters from Africa (now collected in the book *I promise to be good: The Letters of Arthur Rimbaud*), in none of them does he ever make even the slightest reference to (his or any other) poetry. It is as if, for himself, Rimbaud as a poet never existed.

In today's era of hyperconnectivity and mass surveillance (which is, in the end, the same), Rimbaud's big escape would probably have been an impossible task. Either paparazzi would be bombarding us with photos of a naked Rimbaud on a beach in Aden in our daily newspapers, or Twitter and Facebook profiles would be full of statuses about Rimbaud. Today it's impossible to hide.

To recover from the usual hypersocialization effect provoked by another conference, instead of

Rimbaud's big escape, last summer I naively tried to hide on a remote Croatian island, in a lovely old fisherman's town called Komiža.

I arrived at a beach that wasn't especially crowded with people because it was the end of the season. Expecting fewer people there, I headed further down to the nudist beach behind the hills. Unfortunately, the number of people was still too many, so I climbed over unfriendly rocks to reach an even more distant and empty beach.

There it was. No one around. Only me, sitting in the sun and watching the waves lap the shore.

After an hour or so, a small dot appeared on the horizon. When it came closer, I realized it was a man in a kayak. When the kayak landed on the beach, and the man came out of it, I realized he was naked.

Since there was only the two of us, it was normal to start a conversation.

"It is really hot today," he said, looking at the sun.

Then he turned around, standing like Priapus with his large penis in front of my face and asked: "Do you want to cool down?"

"I just had a swim."

"But if you go further, there is a nice cave, haven't you seen it?"

I still didn't see where he was going, so I replied with naive sincerity: "No, I didn't see it yet, and I just wanted to start reading a book."

He became more direct: "Do you want to play?"

Finally, realizing where the whole conversation had been going right from the start; it was just that I didn't get it, I became more direct: "I have a girlfriend."

"I have a girlfriend, too," he responded like a cannon in the middle of the empty beach.

"And you are still playing around?"

"Yes, why not?"

"I do not, and I'm not gay."

"Neither am I, so let's have fun!"

"No!" and a potential summer romance ended here.

Obviously, these days it's impossible to find an empty beach even on the most remote island. Even a while after our pleasant conversation, we were still both sitting on the beach, each in his own small corner of the previously empty beach.

Then, after a short while, another, very small dot appeared on the horizon.

It was a snorkel.

As it came closer, the snorkel transformed into another naked man who soon landed on the beach as well.

Immediately, as if they had an appointment, he lay down beside the other guy, and a few minutes later my untried romance headed in the direction of the alleged cave. Yet another few minutes later, the new guy on the beach put his snorkel back on and swam in the same direction. Who knows, maybe *he* was not interested in having fun with another guy: he actually wanted to talk about his ideas on revolution, and I was the one who took it only as a call for sex.

In the age of "cold intimacies" – a term coined by Eva Illouz to describe the new emotional culture of late capitalism[1] – the encounter is often pre-programmed. In the age of "fuck buddies" people often just become *fuck bodies*. What we encounter today is this sort of liberal permissiveness ("Anything goes!") which is a sad caricature of serious discussions on "free love" between Alexandra Kollontai and V. I. Lenin, or *Kommune 1* and Rudi Dutschke. Already during the October Revolution, Lenin had warned that the demand for freedom of love can be understood as a bourgeois concept, and when the generation of '68 was practicing "free love" at Communes in Berlin, Rudi Dutschke echoed Lenin's words by saying that "the exchange of women and men is nothing else but the application of the bourgeois exchange principle under pseudo-revolutionary auspices."[2]

Isn't the best illustration to be found in Gilbert Adair's novel *The Holy Innocents* (1988) – later put on screen by Bertolucci in his *The Dreamers* – about an erotic triangle set against the background of the '68 Paris student riots? Instead of joining the revolution, what the trio – the incestuous siblings joined by a stranger – does during the whole movie is in a way what was happening in the German *Kommune 1*. Only at the very end of the novel, when the young American student walks away from the '68 chaos, do we see the other two protagonists throwing a Molotov cocktail at the police. Who has won today? It is not these two *enfants terribles*, who were prepared to turn their own sexual lives upside down and at the same time join the riots in the streets, but this young American student who in Adair's novel argued that the riots have no meaning.

The revolutionary aim at changing everyday

life was perverted into the postmodern variety of lifestyles: it is not subversive anymore, at least in the Western world, neither to be gay or a transvestite, nor to have regular sex with two people at the same time or ten. And we have even taken one step further where neither does the content as such have any meaning anymore. It is enough to visit Camden in London or Tarrytown in New York to see where this ideology of lifestyle has brought us: the hipster subculture is the perfect embodiment of this co-optation: it is the pure (hedonistic) aestheticization of everyday life without any subversive potential whatsoever. The "young creatives," although a biography of Che Guevara might be sticking out of their bags, don't even pretend to be doing a revolution of everyday life anymore.

The disastrous consequences of the hyperinflation of this sort of false "reinvention of love" can also be seen in two movies from 2013 which each in its own way tackles the fate of postmodern love affairs. On the one side we have Spike Jonze's *Her*, on the other we have Lars Von Trier's *Nymphomaniac*.

If there is one disturbing moment of this failed "reinvention of love," it is to be found in the moment when the main character in *Her*, Theodore (Joaquin Phoenix), finally tries to compensate for the lack of his computer lover's missing body. When Theodore invites home a real woman in order to have sex with her, a complete stranger arrives accompanied by the voice of Scarlett Johansson (the operating system Theodore is in love with). But instead of successful sex, the abyss between voice and body becomes even more tangible. The effect is not a reunification of body and voice, but complete *alienation*. It is a real "season in hell."

It seems that *Nymphomaniac* is founded on the pure opposite: the never-ending accumulation of bodies – as seen in the first scene when young Joe (Charlotte Gainsbourg) and her friend are competing to see who will fuck more strangers on a moving train. When the "nymphomaniac" exploits hundreds of bodies, she is not disturbed by it. Quite the opposite: the alienating nature of casual sex is exactly what gives her the thrill.

But it would be wrong to think that these two scenes differ so much. What they have in common, even the narcissistic Theodore and the sex animal Joe, is the longing for something that could be characterized as the true Radicality of

Love. Even for the nymphomaniac, the accumulation of fuck bodies inevitably leads to alienation and depression. After all, even the nymphomaniac expresses a need for close emotional contact, although in a sexual form.

Further proof that the nymphomaniac is actually trapped in the commodification and alienation of desire is best illustrated in Steve McQueen's movie *Shame* (2011). Instead of a female nymphomaniac, here we have a young executive in New York (played by Michael Fassbender) who could easily compete with Charlotte Gainsbourg in the infinite accumulation of fuck bodies. During the decadent carnival of various sex experiences (from threesomes to regular hookers and blowjobs in gay clubs), our protagonist surprisingly gets attracted to a beautiful co-worker from his office. They end up on a date in a restaurant where instead of his "sex animal" disguise, we find out that he can be nervous and uncomfortable, even shy. Instead of doing what he would usually do, immediately get someone into bed or just fuck around the corner, he escorts her to the metro station and shyly says "We should do this again" (a date. . .). The next day in the office, he is more confident and kisses her in a hidden corner behind the wall and then brings her to a hotel room where they start with a passionate prelude. But here comes the surprise: at the decisive moment, he can't get an erection. She goes away, he stays at the hotel; the next moment we see him fucking a hooker pressed against the glass of the room window. He couldn't do it with someone he genuinely likes, but he could easily do it a few minutes later with a complete stranger whom he will probably never see again. What we encounter here is the same problem of Charlotte Gainsbourg: when it comes to deeper intimate relationships, it is not that the nymphomaniac doesn't long for it, it is more that he or she is not capable of bonding, of going deeper than just pure sex.

To come back to the encounter on the remote Croatian beach: isn't the meeting of two guys on an empty beach the perfect phantasmatic scenario of recent geosocial networking applications that are invented to "reinvent love," but are merely reinventing "free sex"?

One of the first of such applications was launched in 2009 under the name "Grindr," and it soon exploded into the largest and most popular all-male location-based social network. As the official website states: "With more than 5 million guys in 192 countries around the world – and approximately 10,000 more new users downloading the app every day – you'll always find a new date, buddy or friend."[3]

In his short book *Meet Grindr*, Jaime Woo vividly describes the situation when he first found out about Grindr. It was summer 2009 and he was out on a patio with a group of friends enjoying drinks and the warm weather. They were drinking in the Village, Toronto's main queer neighborhood and queer men were all around them, at the surrounding tables and walking down the street. If any of them wanted a casual encounter, it wouldn't have been difficult.

"But that wasn't the point," explains Woo. "What made Grindr feel revolutionary was the ability to see it all: it was like gaining Superman's X-ray vision, and suddenly being able to peer through brick and steel to reveal all the hungry men around."[4]

But here is the real point: if everything is "*o feet away*," as the official slogan of Grindr states, what about the unrecorded voyages of discovery Rimbaud was speaking about?

To answer this, let us recall one of the most

memorable scenes from Woody Allen's *Annie Hall*: the first meeting between Alvy Singer and Annie on the balcony. While Alvy and Annie try to impress each other with intellectual observations, we see their real thoughts as thought-bubble subtitles at the bottom of the screen.[5]

When Alvy asks Annie whether she did all these photographs, she answers: "Yeah, I sort of dabble around, you know," and we see her real thoughts in subtitles: "I dabble? Listen to me – what a jerk."

Alvy pretentiously replies "Photography's interesting because, you know, it's a new form, and a set of aesthetic criteria have not emerged yet," and we see his real line of thought: "I wonder what she looks like naked."

Annie, on the other hand, is feeling that she lacks self-confidence and is intellectually inadequate and while replying "You mean whether it's a good photo or not?" she really thinks to herself: "I'm not smart enough for him."

In the end, they end up on their first date.

With Grindr this could have been much faster and easier: why bother with such conversations if our real thoughts (or to be more precise: pure drives without any second thoughts) can be visible immediately like Woody Allen's subtitles? Why bother if we have "Superman's X-ray vision"?

Realizing the matchmaking mobile applications could bring an even bigger profit, in 2012 a new application was born called "Tinder," designed for heterosexuals.

Their official website sums up the problem of *Annie Hall*: "Tinder's vision is to eliminate the barriers involved in making new connections and strengthening existing ones." Or as a 20-year-old student Eliel Razon revealed to *Le Monde*: "It is a supermarket, you come, and you do your shopping!"[6]

But is this the real "reinvention of love"? You come and you do your shopping? Shouldn't a real Encounter include a crusade or, sometimes, even a season in hell? What new sexual applications in most cases don't carry is precisely the things that are important in falling in love. Take the empty beach dialogue again: there was no mystery at all, no real encounter at all; only the manifest or metaphorical display of a mating urge without any hidden message. It is as if we had the subtitles from *Annie Hall* without the surface conversation. And this is precisely the biggest problem of Grindr or Tinder: in trying to lead the "real" conversation, you end up in a conversation that is actually much more superficial ("let's fuck").

Again, it is best summed up by Jaime Woo in *Meet Grindr*: "Take the work involved to meet a guy on another site: reading detailed profiles, carefully crafting messages, waiting for responses, and then coordinating a time to meet. Grindr strips this all away: users are presented with a single image, instant message one another if interested, and, since most guys are a quick walk away, can easily meet."

This is the best description of a nightmare. What Grindr's design encourages are rapid transactions between its users to help speed up the discovery of matches. But isn't the point of falling in love precisely the waiting for responses (as shown by Roland Barthes so convincingly in his *Fragments of a Lover's Discourse*), the careful crafting of messages, the coordination to meet . . . Could you imagine Rimbaud falling in love with Verlaine via Grindr? It would probably have an ending like the superbly sarcastic *Love poem* by Banksy from his book *Wall and Piece*.

Today we live in an era of "transparency." Although *nothing* is transparent (we still need

WikiLeaks and Edward Snowden to reveal the non-transparent truths), *everything* is transparent: today we have all sorts of products or innovations that are trying to do things more transparently. Take Microsoft's vision of the "Smart Home" from the now distant 1999 (with biometrics, etc.);[7] or a product called SciO (a molecular sensor that scans relevant information from all sorts of objects);[8] or a cup called "Vessyl" (that automatically tracks everything you drink),[9] and last but not least: the "Electric Eel," an open-source digital condom prototype using electrodes and soft circuitry.[10] This is the future. And, again, it is a nightmare. What we are approaching here is something that the Italian philosopher Franco Berardi (Bifo) in his book *Heroes: Mass Murder and Suicide* calls "trans-human transition" that leads to a "neuro-totalitarianism."[11]

What all these technological innovations have in common is the same logic as Grindr or Tinder. All information is revealed immediately. There is no secret in the world anymore. No wonder a programmer recently invented an application called "Cloak," an antisocial network that helps you to avoid people you don't want to see. "Cloak" came about after Brian Moore moved to

New York and just kept on stumbling into his ex-girlfriend. But it has a more general use as well: "Generally speaking, we feel like we've reached the point of social fatigue – too many networks with too much information, all the time," says Moore.[12]

What is striking in this example is not so much the fact that more and more people are realizing the illness of hyperconnectivity, but that this illness has advanced so much that people who want to get rid of such connections as ex-girlfriends, all sorts of people with whom they are connected via Viber, Facebook, Twitter, Instagram, etc., do it by using the very products that produced their illness in the first place. What is amazing is that Moore didn't arrive at the idea of simply getting rid of his cell phone. For the same reason we can go "invisible" on Skype or Gmail, although we will still be present and still be using the same technology. According to the latest information, "Cloak" already has 300,000+ users and growing.[13] This means going "invisible" nowadays.

And it brings us back to Rimbaud and a wonderful story retold by Charles Nicholl in his biography of Rimbaud's African years (1880–91), *Somebody Else*, which is itself a reference to

Rimbaud's famous *Je est un autre* ("I is some-body else"). The only time during his last 16 years that Rimbaud's true identity was revealed was in 1883, when Alfred Bardey met him on a steamship to Aden. Rimbaud was disguised as a young French journalist, but Bardey had known Rimbaud at college. Not only that, he knew of Rimbaud's growing reputation and the work of "Les Poètes maudits," but Rimbaud's seminal poem "Vowels" had recently been published as well. Nevertheless, Rimbaud pretended to be a journalist on a trip to China, to cover the latest events in Tonkin for *Les Temps*. At some point, Rimbaud's cover was blown, and Bardey realized that it was the great poet. Rimbaud was terrified by the revelation. Later he confessed to Bardey that he received a letter or letters from Verlaine around this time, and that he wrote back just once, with "*Fous-moi la paix*," in other words: "Leave me alone" or "Fuck off."[14]

No traces of these letters survive, but Rimbaud's biographer believes there is no reason to doubt Bardey's reminiscence. There is no reason why we shouldn't believe it too.

Now put this short passage – Rimbaud escap-ing France and his fuck-off letter to Verlaine

– into the context of "Cloak," Grindr and all sorts of other postmodern innovations. Was love really reinvented in our technological era or are we still chased by the *poète maudit*? When we talk about love nowadays, aren't we in most cases merely talking about sex? In the age of "fuck bodies," everyone is a potential "fuck body." But what if what we need instead is a real reinvention of Love?

2

Desire in Tehran:
What Are the Iranians Dreaming Of?

It is early January of 2015 and the streets of Tehran after 10 pm are ghostly empty. All you can see or hear from time to time are the growling motor-bikes passing by like shadows. The Hassan Abad Square, which is usually packed with street ven-dors and women in *chadors* selling wool in the nearby stores, is deserted. It is a square which during the day seems to be impossible to pass through unless you are an integral part of the whole traffic, or looking the drivers directly in their eyes, calculating whether they will slow down or even stop, to everyone's surprise: in Tehran's streets you can easily get the feeling you are like George from a famous *Seinfeld* episode moving through heavy traffic like the frog from the *Frogger* video-game. After 10 pm, you get an entirely different impression.

The ride on the metro, from Taleghani metro station where the (in)famous American Embassy was once based (today decorated with many anti-US murals, like the Liberty of Freedom with the face of a skeleton) to Imam Khomeini metro station, during the evening, looks like a scene from a dystopian movie about deserted cities.

Before the Iranian Revolution, it was quite normal to see people sitting in the streets, drinking tea and smoking *qalyān*; Tehran was full of cafés and cabarets. After the establishment of the Islamic Republic of Iran in 1979, all of these places disappeared, or more precisely, they were forced to close. The small number of remaining cafés can't be seen from the street, as either the windows are darkened or they don't have any, or the cafés are placed in a garden or on the upper floors of a building. To ask why is almost superfluous.

Nonetheless, it deserves an answer: as we know from Richard Sennett's classic book *The Fall of Public Man*, cafés usually have – or at least had or could have – a subversive role. During the ancien régime, political groups often arose from the Parisian cafés. In the years before the

French Revolution, different groups met in Café Procope on the Left Bank, and by the outbreak of the Revolution, every group had their own place. Coffeehouses became not only social centers, but were also the prime *information centers* in London and Paris of the early eighteenth century. So, when Khomeini decided to close the cafés and cabarets, it was because he was fully aware that they might be used as means for (counter-) revolutionary activity.

If you leave Tehran, and come to Shiraz or Yazd in the south of the country, this trend of the disappearance of public space is even more noticeable. Iranian cities are characterized by something we might provisionally describe as "the architecture of walls": if traditional Persian houses usually were built with thick and lofty walls to keep the sun's heat out in summertime and retain internal heat in the winter, now it serves a clear ideological purpose – it seems there is (except in the bazaars) no social life except inside one's house. Not only potentially subversive activities (socializing, gathering and exchanging information, joking about the regime, etc.), but the *very existence of desire* has to be hidden. After all, is there anything more subversive than desire?

As Gilles Deleuze and Félix Guattari point out in their *Anti-Oedipus*:

> If desire is repressed, it is because every position of desire, no matter how small, is capable of calling into question the established order of a society: not that desire is asocial, on the contrary. But it is explosive; there is no desiring-machine capable of being assembled without demolishing entire social sectors. Despite what some revolutionaries think about this, desire is revolutionary in its essence – desire, not left-wing holidays! – and no society can tolerate a position of real desire without its structures of exploitation, servitude and hierarchy being compromised.[1]

This is the reason why dance halls, billiard halls, and swimming pools from the Pahlavi era were also closed immediately following the Iranian Revolution. And does it come as a surprise that Soviet officials also condemned card playing, billiards, and dancing as uncultured and decadent pastimes?[2] It seems these two different revolutions (to be more precise: the Iranian Revolution and the later period of the October Revolution) had something in common: the stance towards desire. Or as Khomeini put it himself in a speech on June 28, 1979:

> Islam prevents lustful behavior. It will not tolerate men and women going swimming together half-naked in the sea. During the period of *taghut*, such things occurred and the women would then go into the towns dressed in their bathing costumes. Today, if they did such a thing, the people would skin them alive.[3]

If Pahlavi's modernization – not only in terms of sexual behavior but also in architecture – was underpinned by an impulse to erase the past (except, of course, Persepolis with which he felt some mystical connection) and create a new modern Iran, it was Khomeini who had a similar impulse but went into the opposite architectural direction: he wanted to erase Pahlavi's past, and return to some mythological *ur*-islam – again, as an act of erasure, but with a return to some non-existent past in which even Persepolis and its legacy (multiculturalism, wine, etc.) was prohibited.

Pahlavi's demolition of residential structures (according to one estimate, between 15,000 and

30,000) was an urban crime,[4] but Khomeini's "architecture of walls" was another, even bigger crime. It went much deeper than urbanism: his revolution was fully aware that architecture is connected to desire as well. It is what Henri Lefebvre, in his forgotten and recently found publication *Toward an Architecture of Enjoyment*, would call "architecture of jouissance." Architecture is always linked to desire. This is the reason why Tehran's post-revolutionary architecture is always directed toward something constantly missing, toward the absent and hidden desire. If the veil hides the sexuality of women, then Tehran's architecture today is designed to hide desire as such.

Just try to put Hundertwasser's advice from his manifesto about the "Window dictatorship and window rights" with his famous "window right" into the Iranian context: a person should be allowed to take a long brush and paint everything outside the window within arm's reach.[5] Of course, this is not possible in the West either, but in Iran this "window right" was perverted into hyper-realistic martyrdom murals all around the cities, sometimes covering whole buildings.[6] In the West we have billboards as our gods, in Iran they have Khomeini and martyrs. If we were to read this "architecture of desire," we might conclude: sacrifice is one of the main ideological fuels of the country, along the lines of Khomeini's famous dictum that "the martyr is the first one to enter paradise" (present at the mural on the wall near the headquarters of the Foundation of Martyrs in Tehran's Taleghani Avenue).

Again, it is the great Khomeini himself who provides us with a cunning explanation:

> A nation that aspires after martyrdom, a nation whose women and men long for martyrdom, who cry out for it, such a nation does not care whether something is in short supply or in abundance. It doesn't let the state of economy bother it, this is for those who are tied to the economy, who have given their hearts to the economy. Those who have given their hearts to God don't care whether something can be found easily on the market or not, whether something is cheap or expensive.[7]

Was there ever a better explanation of the ideological functions of the religious state apparatus? Martyrdom is explicitly defined as an escape from everyday life: who cares how our economy looks if we can become martyrs!

It is the same with Khomeini portraits in all corners of Iran, from official buildings to butchers. You meet Big Brother everywhere, as soon as you exit the airport or enter one of the remaining coffeehouses. Even every rial banknote is covered with his face. And again, this is nothing particular to political Islam; the omnipresence of the Leader wasn't invented in Iran. After Lenin's death, in schools there were established so-called "Lenin Corners," political shrines for the display of the glorious Leader, and it was even worse with Stalin. Even during my childhood, which started in the early 1980s when socialist Yugoslavia had already started to collapse, portraits of Marshal Tito were still present in schools and public institutions. During the 1990s, Tito was replaced by Franjo Tuđman and Slobodan Milošević, the new leaders.

But if the ideological purpose of Lenin's or Tito's portraits lay in the overall belief in progress, which not only looked back nostalgically into the glorious partisan past, but believed in a better future (isn't it best embodied in the economic concept of *pyatiletka* (Five-Year Plans), which we can find only in China today, as one of the main reasons behind China's economic rise?), in Iran, even today, the main purpose of this sort of "production of space" (murals all over the city) is not a future in life, but a future after death. It is as if the purpose of architecture becomes a production of desire for sacrifice.

If we could really – with all caution included – understand the Iranian Revolution as a revolution that propagated the death drive (*Todestrieb*), then it is no surprise that *Eros* has to be oppressed on every corner. The new regime did not restrict itself only to architecture and buildings (universities, schools, public swimming pools, etc.), but went so far as to intervene in the very activities that were taking place inside of these institutions.

As we can find out in Azar Nafisi's *Reading Lolita in Tehran*, even ballet and dancing was banned and the ballerinas were told they had a choice between acting or singing. If it still doesn't sound obscene, just make the following thought experiment: what if you come to a doctor specialized in neurology and propose that he re-specialize in cardiology, or ask a painter to become a cellist? We can imagine that some ballerinas really had to accept this forced choice and became singers, but the regime soon made it even harder for them: women were banned from singing as well. Not only a woman's hair or her dance, but also her voice might be sexually provocative. Again, what we might encounter here is – desire.

The next step was another "logical" step further: the new regime banned all forms of music, except classical and traditional Persian music. No wonder the English punk rock band The Clash released its cult song "Rock the Casbah" in 1982, inspired by Khomeini, with the following line: "by order of the prophet we ban that boogie sound." During the Iranian Revolution revolutionary guards were reported to have organized raids in small villages to find and destroy musical instruments. One explanation was given by one ancient *hadith*: "Listening to music leads to discord, just as water leads to the growth of vegetation," and the other by Khomeini himself in *Keyhan*, Iran's major daily newspaper, during the Revolution: "Music is like a drug, whoever acquires the habit can no longer devote himself to important activities. We must completely eliminate it." Surprisingly or not, it is Lenin – as we will see soon in the following chapters – who had a very similar stance toward music. Everything – from music to love – has to be suppressed if we want the Revolution to succeed.

Since the early days of the Revolution, after closing music schools, even musical instruments have been banned on Iranian TV. Most concerts are also banned. This perversion even goes so far that, when television broadcasts concerts, instruments are not shown and are often replaced with scenes from nature such as flowers or waterfalls. But as always, subversion usually lurks in the cracks of totalitarianism: in January 2014, when being asked to perform live on TV, the popular Iranian jazz-fusion band Pallet subverted this ban by miming instruments during a performance.[8] Legally they didn't break the law, but semiotically the instruments were finally shown.

If there is any field of human activity or appearance that is semiotically directly linked to desire, then it is, of course, fashion. When I arrived in Tehran, among other things in my overloaded inbox I found a link a friend had sent me to an older article about Richard Sennett and Saskia Sassen published in the Italian *Vogue*. There was, as I later found out once I returned to Europe, nothing subversive in it, just a usual fashion magazine item about the sociologist couple and how they share and spend their time (Richard does all the cooking, shopping, and cleaning, etc.). I was surprised when instead of *Vogue*, my internet browser was redirected to a page saying "access to the requested website is not possible," and after a 30-second delay I was redirected to another censorship website, peyvandha.ir. Of course, I was the naïve one: how could I have thought that internet sites related to fashion are not banned in Iran? As Khomeini put it in one of his speeches, fashion was a means "to pervert both our men and our women, to corrupt them and thus prevent them from their human development."[9]

In 2013, a study found that a wide range of websites, not only including sites related to politics, but also to health, science, sports, and – of course – sex are blocked. Almost 50% of the top 500 most-visited websites in the world are blocked, including Facebook, Twitter, and YouTube.[10] A separate study on the Iranian censorship of Wikipedia showed how the regime is blocking URLs and keywords for contents that are perceived as "dirty," "dangerous for societies," or a tool of "seditionists."[11] Again, it is interesting to see which are the most-blocked Wikipedia articles by theme: first are "civil and political contents," second "sex and sexuality." Figure 1 shows the blocked "Sex and sexuality" articles broken down by topic.

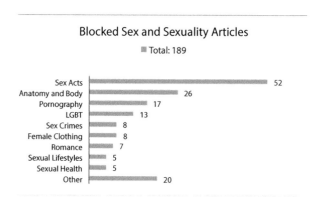

Figure 1 Most-blocked Wikipedia articles under the theme "Sex and sexuality" broken down by topic

In addition to blocking URLs, the regime also blocks keywords. And this often leads to bizarre mistakes: if the character pattern s-e-x is black-listed, the filter will block the website for Essex University (www.essex.ac.uk); articles on Atoll Bikini coral reef in Marshall Islands and on the chemical compound stearalkonium chloride appear to be blocked because they coinciden-tally contained filtered character patterns in their URLs that match sex-related terms; even the page www.no-porn.com, although it promotes overcoming pornography (without any sexual images or explicit text), was blocked by keyword

1. balls / testicles
خایه
خایه

2. bikini
بیکینی

3. bra
سوتین
سوتین

4. breast
پستون

5. clit
چوچوله

6. cock
کیر
کیرش (his cock)
کیری (dickish)

7. cunt
کس

8. curves / butt
قنبل

9. ecstasy
اکستازی

10. fart
گوز
گوزو (farter)

11. fa▮▮t
کونی
کونیم

12. fa▮▮t
کونده

13. fa▮▮ry
همجنسبازی

14. fetish
فتیش
فتیش

15. fucking
گاییدن
گاییدن

16. fucking
گاییدن
گاییدن

17. homo
همجنسباز

18. lesbian
لزبین
لزبین

19. lick / flirtation
لاسیدن
لاسیدن

20. liquor
مشروب

21. penis / wiener
دودول

22. prostitute
فاحشه

23. porn
پورن
پورنو (porno)

24. sex
سکس
سکسی (sexy)

25. sexual desire
شهوانی
شهوانی

26. the thing between
one's legs
لاپایی

27. whore
جنده

28. XXX

Figure 2 The 28 censure keywords identified by analysts, of which 26 were Persian sexual terms or sexual profanities

[handwritten annotation] Interesting that while talking about desire the author blocks out the hate words for homosexuals but not "whore"

54

filtering. Analysts identified 28 censure keywords, of which 26 were Persian sexual terms or sexual profanities, such as the words for "pimp," "dick," "breasts" and "fag" (see Figure 2).

Is this what the Iranians are dreaming of or is it actually the list of wet dreams of the regime itself? One thing is for sure: for a totalitarian system, desire represents a threat: especially the specter of sexual desire ("curves," "butt," "the thing between one's legs," etc.). It is as if Orwell's prophetic words from *Nineteen Eighty-Four* are not only applicable to the Soviet communist regime (after the failed sexual revolution), but could also be applied to the Iranian Revolution: "The sexual act, successfully performed, was rebellion. Desire was thoughtcrime."[12] Why? Because sexual passion, as shown not only in *Nineteen Eighty-Four* (by the character of Winston Smith) but also in Huxley's *Brave New World* (by the character of John Savage), can awake revolutionary impulses. This is the reason why Orwell invented the Anti-Sex League and the Ministry of Love.

As Blu Tirohl argues in his essay "We are the dead . . . you are the dead: An Examination of Sexuality as a Weapon of Revolt in *Nineteen Eighty-Four*," the powerful human instinct which the party transforms into its own fuel is sexual desire:

> The Party, it seems, reappropriates sexual energy for its own needs. As desire, or urge, would diminish after sexual intercourse the Party attempts to sustain in its members a state that permanently anticipates pleasure and then channels that energy for its own purposes.[13]

In Iran desire is noticeable on every corner: sex is everywhere, although it is explicitly seen nowhere. And it is, of course, the woman who is the biggest threat to the stability of the regime. When Orwell describes Julia, in opposition to Winston, it could very well be a description of the Iranian woman:

> She grasped the inner meaning of the Party's sexual puritanism. It was not merely that the sex instinct created a world of its own which was outside the Party's control and which therefore had to be destroyed if possible. What was more important was that sexual privation included hysteria, which was desirable because it could be transformed into war-fever and leader-worship.[14]

In other words, what the regime fears most is the intimate (sex, love . . .) world of its subjects. Or as Julia puts it herself:

> When you make love you're using up energy; and afterwards you feel happy and don't give a damn for anything. They can't bear you to feel like that. They want you to be bursting with energy all the time. All this marching up and down and cheering and waving flags is simply sex gone sour. If you're happy inside yourself, why should you get excited about Big Brother and the Three-Year Plans and the Two Minutes Hate and all the rest of their bloody rot?[15]

Unlike in the most parts of the Western "strip-tease culture,"[16] sex can still be subversive in Iran. Just take the censored keywords, like "balls," "clit," "cock," or "homo" and "lesbian." It is a thoughtcrime. But at the same time, as always, the official *nomenklatura* of the Iranian regime is very cynical itself when it comes to it. For instance, although Iran sentenced eight Facebook users to a combined 127 years in prison for "propaganda" posts in 2014, Iranian President Hassan Rouhani and other members of his administration are very active on Facebook.[17] And wasn't the same sort of double standard of Islamic leaders revealed in the WikiLeaks cables from 2010, which showed how Saudi princes threw parties with drink, drugs, and sex?[18] But like Saudi Arabia, in Iran these joys and desires are also reserved only for the highest stratum of society.

There are plenty of other dirty examples which, again, prove the fact that power elites do have "wet dreams," and at the same time, they do not want others to desire! We could even imagine a cartography or encyclopedia of totalitarian "wet dreams":

1. Muammar Gaddafi. It is well known that music was banned in Libya during his rule. Like in Iran, some instruments were forbidden because they were considered a Western instrument (for instance, the guitar). An Imam in Tripoli even went so far as to give a fatwa in 2008 that encouraged the population to burn all the CDs and cassettes of Arabic and Western music where singers used instruments. And surprise, surprise: already in 1995, another fatwa had been issued, depriving women of their right to sing.[19] But just as in the case

of the Saudi Arabian power elite, this didn't prevent Gaddafi and his family from enjoying (the worst of) Western music. According to documents obtained by WikiLeaks, several pop stars, including Beyoncé, Mariah Carey, Usher, and Lionel Richie have taken lucrative gigs performing for the members of Libyan dictator Muammar Gaddafi's family. After New Year's Eve 2009, Saif al-Islam el-Gaddafi, a son of Col. Gaddafi, had paid Mariah Carey $1 million to sing just four songs at a party on the Caribbean Island of St. Barts.[20] It would be wrong to come to the conclusion that these incidents reveal only the cynicism of the autocratic regimes that use Islam as a cover to realize their own dirty dreams. No, at the same time, it unveils our Western cynicism as well. In principle, nominally, we are all against the suppression of women (in Iran, Libya, Saudi Arabia, etc.), but when it comes to cooperating with these regimes, we don't seem to have a problem! This cynical twist was – yet another time – proven in September 2009 when Gaddafi was supposed to address the UN General Assembly. As we know, the Libyan leader always used large Bedouin tents wherever he went. But sponsoring terrorism or abusing human rights isn't really the best recommendation to allow someone to erect a tent in your backyard. This didn't stop the tycoon Donald Trump from allowing Gaddafi to use an estate belonging to the Trump Organization.[21] OK, now you could say: ah, this is the crazy American tycoon, all of them are the same. But what about the London School of Economics links to Gaddafi? The NGO Gaddafi Foundation pledged to donate £1.5 million over five years to a research center, LSE Global Governance, of which £300k was paid. In addition, LSE Enterprise established a contract worth £2.2 million to train Libyan officials. As a "reward," in 2008 Gaddafi's son, Saif al-Islam Gaddafi, received a PhD from the Department of Philosophy at the LSE with a dissertation entitled "The Role of Civil Society in the Democratization of Global Governance Institutions: From 'Soft Power' to Collective Decision-Making?"[22] If there ever was cynicism embodied, than it is this dissertation title. But the truth of this short passionate affair between the LSE and Gaddafi is to be found in Saif's own words: "Just a few months ago we were being treated as honored friends. Now that rebels are threatening our country, these cowards are turning on us. The way my former friends at the LSE have turned against me and my father is particularly upsetting."[23]

2. Enver Hoxha. Among other things, such as travelling abroad, beards, or kissing on television, the Albanian dictator banned dancing, music, and instruments. According to the BBC article "Dance fever reaches Albania," the mayor of Tirana said that he would cower beneath the bedclothes at night listening to foreign radio stations, an activity punishable by law. He became fascinated by the saxophone. Yet, as such instruments were considered to be an evil influence and were banned, he had never seen one. "Then we heard of a friend who had a saxophone. It was hidden at the bottom of an old trunk belonging to his grandmother," he said.[24] Enver Hoxha explained it in his own words at the Plenum in October 1965, when the situation of literature and arts in Albania was discussed and orientations for their further development were given: "The theatre, the ballet, the variety shows, the opera cannot be at service of those

who are sick in the head, but of those whose heads are in order and whose hearts beat in unison with the heart of the people."[25]

3. Saparmurat Niyazov. In April 2001 he banned foreign opera and ballet. He justified his decision on the grounds that such cultural forms were "alien" to Turkmen culture. He banned circuses, loud mobile-phone conversation (actually a good measure!), music in cars, and abolished – or better to say, reinvented – the calendar (a measure of every true revolutionary!). But the European Union didn't have a problem doing business with him. Why? Because of Turkmenistan's high reserves of natural gas and business opportunities (investments, mainly in real estate and construction).

Here we should stop. Otherwise, we might go on forever with this inexhaustible list of obscenities (from Idi Amin to Kim Jong Il). What we can see from all these examples is the following: although nominally it prescribes and prohibits desire, the totalitarian regime actually does this in order to keep the *joussance* for itself. Fear lies in the fact that others could somehow desire, or even fulfill their desires, too! As a result, what such control of desire creates is a society in which only the (powerful, or rich) elites can have access to nominally denounced desires.

I had the luck to encounter this already on the very first day of my visit to Tehran. Dining in the traditional teahouse Azari, on the corner of Vali-E-Asr Avenue and Raahahan Square, you can without disturbance watch the performance of – something that was supposed to be – "traditional Persian music" and smoke *qayrlal*. But no alcohol included, of course. Surprisingly, a family at the other table, after offering to pay for our dinner, asks: ". . . and can we invite you to our home as well?" Driving a Mercedes with leather seats, our host, with a satisfied smile on his face, pulls out a bottle of vodka. Streets are even emptier than before, almost no cars around at midnight.

Once we are at their family home, the parents of Farrokh are already there. Before crossing their threshold, they tell us: "It is a custom here in Iran to take off shoes." Later they jokingly admit it's not because of tradition, but because of their Persian carpet worth $11,000. Except serving traditional nuts, they immediately ask whether we would like to drink vodka or whiskey. Whiskey it is. After tasting a glass of Grant's, Nasrine asks me: "And . . . is it fake or original?" I answer: "It tastes original," and her whole presence turns into a smile. Not only are expensive cars or carpets perceived as a social marker, but the very possibility of being able to drink (quality) alcohol is also a status symbol in Iran.

Nasrine, who is the wife of Farrokh, is a perfect example of the Janus-like Iran today. On the one hand, in public, she wears the veil; as soon as she enters the car, she removes it. As one of the modern women similar to Nasrine admits to the Iranian-American anthropologist Pardis Mahdavi in her book *Passionate Uprisings: Iran's Sexual Revolution*, for them to speak Persian and wear proper clothes in front of their conservative parents, and go out with friends and speak English and wear sexy clothes is "like drinking water. We dress and act a certain way on the street and a different way in the home; if it wasn't like this we would find it strange."[26]

And this is a good point: if they would have been completely identified with the regime's ideological (per)version of Islam, they would have a serious problem. Just like in good old Yugoslavia, a person who is completely identified with socialism, i.e. sincerely believing in it, would be considered a fool – or even potentially dangerous.[27]

On the other hand, if wearing and removing the veil is just nothing more than lifestyle, then we encounter an even bigger problem. This double life – *zāher/bāten* (outer self/inner self) divide – doesn't have to be understood as subversive per se. Of course, it can be subversive in a country where you have signs in the metro "Women only" or advice in hotels "Please obey the Islamic dress code," but on the other hand it can also lead into a new passivization. In the case of the *nouveau riche*, it leads to a classical type of commodity fetishism and commodification of desire. Our freedom to be different than the regime's vision of us, to transgress the rules and establish our own hidden ways of life, ends up in the liberty to consume and in the end perfectly strengthens the system and its hypocritical ideology.

Isn't this hypocrisy best embodied in the apocryphal episode when Khomeini provided a profound solution to the problem of a man who has had sex with a chicken? In his *Clarification of Problems*, similar to the *responsa* ("answers") of Roman jurisprudence, the students of Khomeini noticed the following astonishing answer: "Neither the man nor his immediate family, not even a next-door neighbor can eat the chicken, but it is okay for a neighbor who lives two doors away to eat that chicken."

Isn't this obscene hypocrisy at its purest: so, it is okay to penetrate a chicken, but it is not okay to eat it unless you live two doors away? Obviously, the real problem is not sex with a chicken, but eating the chicken after sex.

Even if it is an apocryphal episode, isn't Khomeini's solution to "chicken sex" what characterizes Iranian society today? Although something that shouldn't be considered "perverse" is strongly prohibited (women's hair, dance, voice, etc.), the really perverse things (such as fucking a chicken, putting portraits of martyrs on every lamppost, Khomeini in every room, etc.) are regarded as morally acceptable values. This is one of the reasons why Iran is a two-faced society and almost everyone is leading at least a double life.

And the same goes for alcohol. Although alcohol is strongly forbidden, Iranians are the third highest consumers of alcohol in Muslim-majority Middle Eastern countries, behind Lebanon and

Turkey (in both of which it is legal to drink). Iran is full of such "contradictions." It always has two faces: when you visit the tomb of the fourteenth-century poet Hafez in Shiraz, you can see many young people inspiringly reciting poems of their legendary poet, but it is precisely Hafez who lauded the joys of love and wine. There is a saying in Iran that there are two books in every household – one is the Koran and the other Hafez. The first is read, the other is obviously not. Because if Hafez would be read correctly, the very act of reading him would already be considered subversive; just take the following verse: "Drunkards we are by a divine decree, By the special privilege of heaven, Foredoomed to drink and foreordained forgiven" or "Connect the heart to the wine, so that it has body, then cut off the neck of hypocrisy and piety of this new man."[28]

Finally, after they insisted on drinking the whole bottle of whiskey, and we were leaving their home, Nasrine and Farrokh warn us to look down in front of the apartment's entrance. And there it is, the last surprise: a logo of Versace in Farsi inscribed into the ground.

And here is one of the first possible answers to the question of what Iranians are dreaming of today. If it is not the Ayatollah, then it is, even if they are not aware of it, the freedom to consume – not only products, but different lifestyles; the Imaginary West. During the time of Yugoslavia, Kinder Surprise Eggs or Haribo Gummy Bears, which were regularly brought by Yugoslav emigrants (*Gastarbeiter*), weren't only perceived as a much-desired commodity, but as a symbol of the prosperous West and its freedom of choice. Soon, immediately after the fall of Yugoslavia, when the so-called "Transition" period (from socialism to capitalism) started, we found out you need money in order to choose. And once we finally entered the European Union (at least Slovenia and Croatia did), we soon realized that all that we took for granted during socialism was now rapidly privatized: you can choose education and health insurance, but it is not free anymore, as it was in Yugoslavia. You can choose only if you can afford your choice; this is now freedom of choice. What we understood as the freedom to choose was nothing more than freedom to consume, to invest, even in your education, health, etc. This is the "participation society" Dutch King Willem-Alexander announced in September 2013 when he proclaimed that the welfare state of the twentieth century is gone. Instead of relying on the national government, people must take responsibility for their own future and create their own social and financial safety nets. Willem-Alexander said that nowadays, people expect and "want to make their own choices, to arrange their own lives, and take care of each other."[29] But as always: life is good for those who can quickly accommodate themselves to this new *modus vivendi*. Not everyone can make a choice.

For the Iranian *nouveau riche* life is good in Iran. Our hosts were a typical example of the recent (late capitalist) development of the Islamic Republic: they made a fortune in the air-conditioning business and besides drinking alcohol at home, they travel a lot, from Venice to Paris, wear international fashion brands, smoke Western cigarettes, etc.

Of course, for them this might look like freedom, but is this "freedom" really *freedom*? We will try to answer this in one of the upcoming chapters on the legacy of '68. For now, let's put it in short: the double-faced Iranian *nouveau riche* is in no way opposed to the theocratic regime and its limits to personal *freedoms* – because they can afford with money what they consider to be

69

interesting that limiting their consumption is the gov. way of controlling desire while in our country we are consumer based and are pushed to desire "freedom." The Islamic republic as such doesn't seem to have any problems with Western capitalism: although you can still see anti-American murals at the former American Embassy or on some other buildings in Tehran, you can find Coca-Cola, Nestlé or other Western brands almost everywhere. Even the bazaar is now full of fake Western brands or cheap Chinese goods.

It is the bazaar where we accidentally encounter H. the next day.

H. is the pure opposite of the *nouveau riche* family we have been socializing with the evening before. He is even the opposite of the traditional and still-prevailing type of Iranian *bazaaris*.[30] Although the *bazaaris* are traditionally known as the most reactionary force in Iran (when Khomeini was supposed to come back to Iran, they were the ones who even rented a Boeing 747, including fuel and crew), the situation has changed in the meantime – or at least seems to be changing. Now it is no longer surprising that strikes spread around bazaars in Iran from time to time: for example, the strike at the bazaar in Tehran in 2010 against new tax regulations, or in 2012 when the *bazaaris* went on strike again because of Ahmadinejad's economic policy and the falling currency. Of course, one of the interpretations might be that these strikes still don't prove that the *bazaaris* are not reactionaries anymore (protesting against the economic reforms or falling currency can be understood as just another way to protect their own privileges), but then, in October 2014, something extraordinary happened in the bazaar of Esfahan: merchants and shopkeepers refused to open their shops in protest against the acid attacks connected with the revolutionary guards on women's faces (in early October 2014 alone, there were as many as 14 acid attacks on young women in Esfahan, because they were "badly veiled" or were wearing "improper" clothes).[31] This is one face of the bazaar today. And it is not surprising that even the so-called "Arab Spring" was sparked by a young Tunisian street vendor – Mohamed Bouazizi – who set himself on fire on December 17, 2010. Can this be the engine or at least spark off change?

H. says confidently: "One day there will be an explosion in Iran."

"In Iran people don't live, they just move," he adds in a much more pessimistic tone.

"How do you mean?"

"Like vampires, or ships . . . they are just moving around. They don't live."

H. gives a succinct and calm explanation, devoid of any melancholy for the "good old times" (for him the Shah was not a better option either): "Once, Tehran alone had more than 20 cabarets. Today you can't even buy Beethoven, you must search for it on the black market."

"If Beethoven is subversive, what then about books? For instance, someone who is quite popular again in the West – Marx?"

"Ah, Marx . . . not even *Who's Afraid of Virginia Woolf?* or Stendhal."

"And what about theater? Is there, except several state theaters, any real alternative or even underground theater?"

"For theater you need a stage. And underground theater is impossible, as soon as you would start to perform in homes, the regime would notice something strange is happening, people are regularly gathering."

For H., Iran represents a country where everything is hidden; this is why "people live two lives simultaneously."

"There is no freedom in a state where you can't go to the cinema or opera."

I ask him whether he might be in trouble for such harsh words.

H. answers: "Yes."

"And can you be in trouble because of speaking with us?"

"Yes, and I don't know if I can trust you."

"But how do you then survive in such a world?"

H. says: "There is a saying: yard by yard, life is hard. Inch by inch, life's a cinch. If you just look to the distant future, life might seem hard, but if you work day by day and live the moments, it's like drinking water."

I ask him whether this is his shop.

"I suppose so," and H. points in the direction of the entrance and says someone tried to burn it down just a few days ago.

Every word has a deeply thought-out weight, but H. pronounces them so easily, without any resentment. How can something be perceived as *your* shop if it can burn down any day, if everything is uncertain?

He is the pure opposite of the above described *nouveau riche*. He has been to London and Paris, visited exhibitions, opera, but he doesn't perceive freedom as a banal right to choose between different products or lifestyles.

"But I have to warn you, neither in Europe do we have freedom anymore," I said.

H. answers: "At least you can choose if you want to go to the cinema or opera?"

"Yes, but more and more it is the case that we can't choose when it comes to the really important things, such as free health care or free education. You can choose, but only if you have money."

H. listens carefully, but is not impressed. For him this is still more than the Iranian freedom. For him the first elementary level of (negative) freedom is to be free of religion or nation: neither Shah Pahlavi nor Khomeini. He is sure better times for Iran will come.

So, what are the Iranians dreaming of today, to pose the same question as Foucault did during the Iranian Revolution? As we could see, some of them are dreaming the same dream as Khomeini (*chadors*, segregation of men and women, moral police, martyrdom, etc.), some of them are dreaming the dream of Pahlavi (jet-set life and the free market with a strong state); and some of them – who according to H. are not a minority – are dreaming of a different sort of freedom.

This freedom is not about going to a café or

cabaret, it is about the very possibility that you can do it if you really want. Of course, for the cynical left from the West that might sound like a "liberal dream" that ended up in what Renata Salecl would call the "tyranny of choice," but for the Iranians who are dreaming a different dream than Khomeini's or Pahlavi's, this means the first step toward the very possibility of freedom. When the explosion erupts in Iran, one thing is for sure: it will have to face more than a three-decade-long process of regulating desire (sex and love, etc.) in the everyday lives of Iranians, be it women, men . . . or chickens.

To paraphrase Ryszard Kapuściński from his beautiful account of the Iranian revolution in *Shah of Shahs*: everyone is living on top of a volcano these days again, and anything could set off the eruption.

3

Libidinal Economy of the October Revolution

If we want to know what could happen when it comes to a real – and not reactionary like Khomeini's – explosion, we should go further back in the revolutionary history of the twentieth century and look at the beginning of the October Revolution. It was an eruption of desire; when it comes to *Thanatos*, it was an explosion in the opposite direction to the Iranian Revolution. At least at the very beginning. The tragedy of the October Revolution is that it ended almost like the Iranian Revolution – in a totalitarian society of the suppressing of emotions.

At the very beginning, the October Revolution brought not only tremendous changes in property rights, religion, etc., but a sexual revolution as well. Engels couldn't be more right when he said that "it is a curious fact that with every great revolutionary movement the question of 'free love' comes in to the foreground'."[1] (And maybe this is the measure of a "great revolutionary movement" and a possible answer why today the question of "free love" is missing: because there is no great revolutionary movement?) Wilhelm Reich, who was a witness to the profound changes in sexuality during Soviet times, claims along the lines that "from the course of the Russian revolution, we must learn that economic revolution, expropriation of private ownership of the means of production, and political establishment of a social democracy (dictatorship of the proletariat) automatically go hand in hand with a revolution in attitudes toward man's sexual relationship."[2]

Having this in mind, it really doesn't come as a surprise that the beginning of the October Revolution was marked by a sexual revolution that involved some of the most progressive family and gender legislation that the world had ever seen. Two of Lenin's edicts, proclaimed on December 19 and 20, 1917 ("On the Dissolution of Marriage" and "On Civil Marriage, Children and Civil Registration") opened up the space for abolishing the inferior position of women under law, permitted divorce and abortion, allowed women to retain full control over their property and earnings after marriage, etc. But how and why has this huge emancipatory energy vanished? How was the terrain opened so that the law against homosexuality could be reintroduced in the Soviet Union already in June 1934, along with abortion being outlawed and divorce legislation being renewed?

To answer these questions we must go back to the early 1920s, to one of the most influential early Soviet commentators on sex. Aaron Zalkind – the psychoneurologist who attempted to synthesize the work of Freud, Pavlov, and Marx, and the leader of "psychohygiene," arguing that the body had been "disorganized" by capitalism – claimed that the market economy had given rise to conditions that had "sexualized the universe" and that capitalism uses sex as a new opiate for the masses (if we have Grindr or Tinder in mind, or *Fifty Shades of Grey*, we might agree). Zalkind started from a similar position as Wilhelm Reich: capitalism restrains primal sexual instincts and thus a political revolution needs to get rid of the constraints of bourgeois sexual morality. However,

Zalkind and Reich are the best examples of two people who have had the same starting point but arrive at completely opposite conclusions.

For Zalkind, the only cure for the new revolutionary subject (the "New Man") is to be found in sexual abstinence: what we need is asceticism and not the complete release of accumulated sexual tensions of the organism (Reich's "orgastic potency"). Does it then come as a surprise that, in the second part of his *The Sexual Revolution* under the title "Struggle for the 'New Life' in the Soviet Union," Reich complains that the Soviet Union, after the first revolutionary period of Lenin's era, has become reactionary in terms of sex politics and "sex-economic regulation"?

Wilhelm Reich visited Moscow in September 1929, where he gave several lectures and even visited a number of kindergartens and child-care centers, but instead of finding progressive sexual policy, he was disappointed that many educators had the same "bourgeois" moralistic attitudes about childhood sexuality as their colleagues in capitalist countries. He was impressed by certain measures from the early revolutionary era – legalized abortion, simple divorce, "children's collectives," etc. – but he found signs indicating that by 1929 the Soviet Union was already beginning to retreat from this revolutionary breakthrough.

In the preface to the second edition of *The Sexual Revolution*, in 1936, he gives the best summary of the problem:

> Owing to confusion about the laws of sexuality, Communism has tried to retain the form of bourgeois morality while changing its content; thus a 'new morality' is produced in the Soviet Union, displacing the old one. This is erroneous. Just as state does not merely change its form but 'wither away' completely (Lenin), so compulsory morality, too, does not merely change but wither away.[3]

To get a taste of this new "libidinal economy," we should take a glance at the bizarre agitational drama *Sexual Depravity on Trial* published in 1927 by Dr E. B. Demidovich, the physician who had warned of the evil effects of masturbation. Zalkind himself endorsed it by writing a preface for it and praising the role of fictional trials as a tool for highlighting sexual questions and arousing the consciousness of the youth. Later, these "pedagogic" sexual fictional trials would, of course, become the main tool for eliminating political enemies (so-called "show trials"). The central point of the play concerns the dilemma whether a man can be charged with abandoning his wife, given the official policy of free marriage and divorce in the USSR: The *bon vivant* Semyon Vasiliev abandonded his wife Anna Vtorova, who was three months pregnant; his sexual behavior led to disastrous social consequences including syphilis and abortion. Anna's brother appears in court as the principal accuser. He is a Party member for several years and the pure representative of the healthy and strong youth.

Defense Attorney (D): Witness Vtorov, you, it seems, are twenty-three years old.

Vtorov (V): Yes, twenty-three.

D: Are you married?

V: No, I'm not.

D: Well, and how do you approach women?

V: Like a comrade.

D: And how do you part with them?

V: Also like a comrade.

D: You've had children?

V: Me?. . . No, I haven't.

D: You've used birth control?

V: Never.

D: So you are not healthy?

V: I am absolutely healthy . . . I have never had a sex life.

D: At twenty-three years of age?

V: At twenty-three years of age.

D: I have no further questions.

Expert (E): May I pose several questions to the witness?

Judge: By all means.

E: You have experienced attraction to a woman?

V: Yes.

E: What has held you back from intimacy?

V: I am a member of the Party. I need strength for the construction of a new form of life and I strive conscientiously so that my sex life does not cripple me, or a woman, or our child. I am young and won't need a woman any time soon, and I am looking for one who will attract me not for a day and not for a month, but for many years. I am looking for a woman who would be both a woman and a comrade-in-work.

E: And so far you haven't found one?

V: Sometimes it has seemed as if I have. But upon checking it's been clear that it was a mistake.

E: And how do you check?

V: I simply wait, allow the attraction to strengthen, observe her and myself, asking myself do I want a child with her.

E: And is that all that restrains you?

V: No, it's not all. I conscientiously want to begin a sex life only when a child will not frighten me.

E: Is the battle difficult?

V: It's easier in the winter. In the summer it's harder, especially at the beginning.

E: Do you suffer from insomnia?

V: No, I sleep splendidly.

E: What helps you in the battle?

V: Breaks for physical exercise. I try to avoid being alone when I have free time. Social work helps me a lot. When nature rebels, I inconspicuously avoid girls. When I am calm again I spend time with them once more.[4]

As we can see, this is the ideal Komsomol member: although he is 23 years old, he is still a virgin; when he has a sexual urge, he participates in sports; in order to avoid masturbation he even avoids solitude. He is just another version of Rakhmetov from Chernyshevsky's *What Is To Be Done?*, the "rigorist" character who avoids women and all other potential sources of pleasure, gymnastics and sports, and even sleeps on a bed of nails as his final act of self-discipline. These are the ideals of the "new morality." It could have jumped straight out of Khomeini's kitchen.

In his book *Sex in Public: The Incarnation of Early Soviet Ideology*, Eric Naiman provides us with even more bizarre examples of the rhetoric in the Soviet Union during the 1920s. Dr M. Lemberg, writing in 1925, recommended five rules for avoiding sexual stimulation:

1. Never drink alcohol.
2. Sleep on a hard bed. Upon waking stand up at once.
3. Don't eat too much meat. Eat three hours before sleep. Urinate before going to bed.
4. Don't read erotic literature
5. Don't lead a sedentary life.[5]

At first glance it might sound like moral commandments from the Iranian Revolution. If the "hero" of *Sexual Depravity on Trial* fought against sexual drives by physical exercise and by avoiding being alone, Dr Lemberg was even more specific and even proposed correct nutrition before sleeping. Why is insomnia a problem? Because in the silence of the night, sexual thoughts might appear. And if you read erotic literature before sleeping, the chances are even greater that you could get an erection.

It would be strange if one of the most important figures of this "new morality" wasn't engaged in similar prescriptions. Aaron Zalkind went a step further and provided us with "twelve commandments," most of them phrased in the negative as well:

1. Sexual life should not begin too early.
2. Sexual abstinence is essential until marriage, and marriage should occur only when full social and biological maturity has been reached (age twenty to twenty-four).
3. Sexual intercourse should only be the culmination of profound mutual affection and of attachment to the sexual object.
4. The sexual act should be the final link in a chain of profound and complex experiences uniting lovers.
5. The sexual act should not be repeated often.
6. Sexual partners should not be changed frequently.
7. Love should be monogamous.

8. At every sexual act, the possibility that progeny will result should always be remembered.

9. Sexual selection should occur in accordance with class and Revolutionary proletarian selection. Flirtation, courtship, coquetry, and other methods of specifically sexual conquest should not enter into sexual relations.

10. There should be no jealousy.

11. There should be no sexual perversion.

12. In the interests of Revolutionary expediency a class has the right to interfere in the sexual life of its members. Sexuality must be subordinated to class interests; it must never interfere with them and must serve them in all respects.[6]

All these examples – the fictional court trials, Dr Lemberg's rules, and finally, the "twelve commandments" – exemplify one of the main foundations of the new libidinal economy: *energy saving*. The main complaint against sexuality is that it represents too much expenditure of energy, which prevents the individual from contributing to society ("sexuality must be subordinated to class interests"). Sexual energy is thus conceived as a working-class resource that should be preserved for the sake of proletarian creativity and production (even "flirtation, courtship, coquetry and other methods of specifically sexual conquest" should be avoided).

It is a problem that was, as always, best summed up by Roland Barthes in his interview for *Playboy* in 1977:

> The lover is himself the site of a fierce investment of energy, and he therefore feels himself excluded from other investments of a differing nature. The only human being with whom he could feel complicity would be another lover. After all, it's true that lovers understand each other! But a political militant is, in his fashion, in love with a cause, an idea. And this rivalry is unendurable. On either side. I don't think a political militant could easily put up with someone madly in love . . ."[7]

And it is here that we return once more to Lenin. The widespread hypertrophy in sexual matters was dangerous because people might say "gentle things" instead of working for the revolution, and this is why Lenin – in his response to Clara Zetkin – insisted that the youth should devote themselves to healthy sport, swimming, walking, and bodily exercise. Even Lenin's famous stance towards the *Appassionata* is in this regard to be taken as suppression of the sexual energy that now has to be sublimated and preserved for the building of socialism.

If we were to sum up the fundamental fear of the early socialist *nomenklatura*, then it would be precisely the fear of energy consumption; the fear of wasting energy into libidinal investments that could be used for the building of the new socialist society. In this context, it comes as a self-fulfilling prophecy that Lenin's death in 1924 was caused by a cerebral hemorrhage that, according to most experts, was provoked by his excessive work for the revolution (it is well known that, when in good health, Lenin worked 14–16 hours each day!). As Dr V. N. Rozanov, the physician who treated Lenin after the attempt on his life in 1918, said: "Undoubtedly, Vladimir Ilich's death was exclusively produced by the fact that he gave absolutely all of his strength to the service of the interests of the working people." Nikolai Semashko, the minister of health and the one who proposed to "export" Lenin's brain to Berlin for study, claimed his death came about because he did not save his strengths and worked his entire life.

In this respect, Wilhelm Reich's advice to comrade Lenin could have been the following: by falling into the underworld of lower passions such as sex from time to time, you could have achieved your energy balance! In other words, it is precisely by sex that you could have been more useful for the revolution! Moreover, a retrospective diagnosis published in *The European Journal of Neurology* in 2004 says the cause of Lenin's death had come from the realm of these lower passions – from syphilis![8]

Whatever the real reason behind Lenin's death might be, one thing is for sure: it served again to stress how the "new man" has to commit completely to the society he is trying to build. And it is precisely here where the main reason for the "retarding of the sexual revolution" can be found. According to Reich, on the one hand the germ of this regression lay in the rise of concepts of conservative sexology, mainly the idea that sexuality is antithetical to sociality and that sexual life is a "diversion from the class struggle."

On the other hand, there was an objective factor preventing the full development of the sexual postulates of early 1917: since the revolution didn't succeed in bringing economic prosperity (only famine, prostitution, etc.), it was also hard to fulfill the ideals of "sexual freedom" under these circumstances. What happened to the sexual revolution present in Lenin's 1917 edicts was a slow and continuous regression, supported and realized by the official instruments of the Party.

But: it would be wrong to think that from the beginning the outcome of this struggle was clear. The discussions about sexuality were really disparate, until two main waves developed and ultimately confronted one another: on the one hand, the "demand for free love," insisting on the argument that only more emancipation could help the revolution and create a classless society, and, on the other, the more conservative current gathered around figures such as Zalkind, who promoted a perverse puritanism and sublimation of sexual drives.

If the economic revolution goes hand in hand with the sexual revolution, then it is no wonder that the libidinal economy went in the more conservative direction when the real economy was faced with the trap of its own obstacles and contradictions. The ideology of sexual abstinence and sublimation soon became mainstream and the official ideology of the Soviet State.

One of the main instruments from the very beginning – already when the Bolsheviks seized power in 1917 – was the spread of didactic, theatrical, and fictional (even fantastical) trials not only published but also performed in workers' and soldiers' clubs in the years from 1919 to 1933. We shouldn't underestimate the role of these didactic trials. As Lynn Mally shows in *Revolutionary Acts: Amateur Theater and the Soviet State*, it was the amateur theater that helped to legitimize the Soviet state.[9] And it is no wonder that already in 1919 the motto of the new state's cultural ministry was "theater is the self-educator of the people."

The topics of these show trials ranged from the bad effects of smoking cigarettes or sexual diseases (so-called "sanitation trials"), to hooliganism or responsibilities of women in the home. Already by looking at the titles of these didactic trials, we can see that the conservative shift started pretty early. In late 1922 typical titles included *The Trial of a Prostitute* or *The Trial of Citizen Kiselev Accused of Infecting His Wife with Gonorrhea Which Resulted in Her Suicide*. In 1926 a play under the title *The*

Trial of a Husband Who Beat His Wife While in a Drunken State was performed.

Most of these fictional court cases were directed against sexual promiscuity. For instance, the famous Komsomol novel by Nikolai Bogdanov, *First Girl* (1928), about a girl named Sanya, centers around the same topic. Sanya is a Komsomol member who is rewarded for her heroism in the civil war and sent to Moscow, where she promptly becomes involved with several men, infecting each with syphilis. At the end Sanya is shot dead by an uninfected comrade. On the other hand, the promiscuous heroine of Sergei Malashkin's *Moon's on the Right Side* (1926) can't even remember how many dozens of lovers she's had, because saying "no" to the *tovarishchi* might be considered bourgeois.

While the Imaginary of the 1920s was full of sexual adventure, promiscuity, unwanted pregnancy, and transmitted diseases, it ultimately led to the quelling of debate in the 1930s through the harsh Reality of Stalinism. After the short-lived sexual revolution in Soviet literature, now comes socialist realism, with the new communist hero Pavel Korchagin from Ostrovsky's *How the Steel Was Tempered* (1934) proclaiming the new credo of this epoch: "Mama, I've sworn to myself not to chase girls until we've knocked off the bourgeoisie in the whole world." And couldn't we imagine an Islamic fundamentalist (9/11, *Charlie Hebdo*, ISIS, etc.) saying the same thing? (Although here the twist consists in the fact that chasing girls is permitted in heaven. One of the most bizarre stories from the Iran-Iraq War are the so-called "human wave" attacks, organized by the Islamic Republic of Iran, in order to sweep for land mines and absorb Iraqi heavy artillery. In order to encourage young people to die, they were given plastic keys, ostensibly good for opening the door to heaven and erotic delights.)

Of course, it didn't mean that the heated debate completely disappeared. It is enough to read the brilliant Mayakovsky's satirical play – a science fiction *par excellence* (but like every good SF, a *Verfremdungseffekt*-critique of the actual existing regime) – *The Bedbug* from 1929, that gives a rather unflattering portrayal of future socialist society. This future didn't only eradicate human vices such as alcoholism, swearing, and bourgeois thoughts. No, it also prohibited Love. At one point in the play, a reporter talks about a poor girl who began to go out of her mind:

Her parents were heartbroken and called in the doctors. The professors say it's an acute attack of an ancient disease they called 'love'. This was a state in which a person's sexual energy, instead of being rationally distributed over the whole of his life, was compressed into a single week and concentrated in one hectic process. This made him commit the most absurd and impossible acts.[10]

Love has become an illness. Another girl covers her face with her hands and says "I'd better not look. I can feel these 'love' microbes infecting the air!" and the reporter replies: "She's finished, too. The epidemic is taking on oceanic proportions." Forget Ebola, be afraid of Love!

Among the fears of the new socialist society wasn't only the enemy from outside (Western capitalism, the Germans, etc.), but also an enemy within, much more dangerous, because he is invisible, almost like in the *Invasion of the Body Snatchers* – it is the same enemy as the enemy of the Iranian Revolution: *desire*.

As expected, *The Bedbug* (directed by Vsevolod Meyerhold, with music composed by the young Dmitri Shostakovich) met a range of hostile reactions ("too few positive heroes," "an unfavourable view of a future Soviet society," etc.). In January 1930 a seminar took place in Moscow with the title "Do we need Satire?" The conclusions: satirical work has an anti-Soviet form and the class enemy can very easily disguise himself by employing satire. *The Bedbug* didn't stay long in the repertoire and Mayakovsky himself ended up as the poor girl from his play.

As we can see, not only sex, but love as such was one of the central topics of the October Revolution. In her *Reminiscences of Lenin*, published after Lenin's death, Clara Zetkin reveals that Lenin frequently spoke about the women's question as an essential part of the communist movement. But once, when they tackled the question of prostitution and how prostitutes could be organized for the revolutionary fight, Lenin started to criticize Clara Zetkin and the women's movement by saying,

> Your list of sins, Clara, is still longer. I was told that questions of sex and marriage are the main subjects dealt with in the reading and discussion evenings of women comrades. They are the chief subject of interest, of political instruction and education. I could scarcely believe my ears when I

heard it. The first country of proletarian dictatorship surrounded by the counter-revolutionaries of the whole world, the situation in Germany itself requires the greatest possible concentration of all proletarian, revolutionary forces to defeat the ever-growing and ever-increasing counterrevolution. But working women comrades discuss sexual problems and the question of forms of marriage in the past, present and future.[11]

What we can see here is that Lenin, although he was interested in the women's question and even a fierce supporter of it, when it came to more radical questions such as prostitution or sex, couldn't understand why they are of such importance. The biggest problem he saw in it was the following one: it wasn't the right time to amuse proletarian women with discussions on love. Now all thoughts of women comrades had to be directed toward the proletarian revolution. Lenin perceived himself as a "gloomy ascetic" and he understood the so-called new sexual life of the youth to be purely bourgeois, as an extension of bourgeois brothels: it had nothing in common with "freedom of love" as the communists understand it.

It is precisely here that Lenin elaborates his critique of Alexandra Kollontai, although never mentioning her by name:

> You must be aware of the famous theory that in communist society the satisfaction of sexual desire, of love, will be as simple and unimportant as drinking a glass of water. The glass of water theory has made our young people mad, quite mad (. . .) I think this glass of water theory is completely un-Marxist, and moreover, anti-social. In sexual life there is not only simple nature to be considered, but also cultural characteristics, whether they are of a high or low order (. . .) Of course, thirst must be satisfied. But will the normal man in normal circumstances lie down in the gutter and drink out of a puddle, or out of a glass with a rim greasy from many lips? But the social aspect is the most important of all. Drinking water is of course an individual affair. But in love two lives are concerned, and a third, a new life, arises. It is that which gives it its social interest, which gives rise to a duty towards the community. As a communist I have not the least sympathy for the glass of water theory, although it bears the fine title "satisfaction of love". In any case, this liberation of love

is neither new, nor Communist. You will remember that about the middle of the last century it
was preached as the "emancipation of the heart" in
romantic literature. In bourgeois practice it became
the emancipation of the flesh.[12]

Lenin didn't mean to preach asceticism by his
criticism: communists will not bring asceticism,
but: joy of life, power of life – and a satisfied love
can help to do that. However, the widespread
hypertrophy of sexual matters was dangerous.
Instead of this, "young people should devote
themselves to healthy sport, swimming, racing,
walking, bodily exercises of every kind and intellectual interests." Instead of the "freedom of
love," we need self-control and self-discipline
because the struggle to maintain and strengthen
the Soviet power was far from ended.

During this heated discussion Lenin asked
Clara Zetkin to report on and discuss the matter
at a meeting of leading woman comrades and
added: "It's a pity, a great pity, that Comrade
Inessa is not here."[13]

Inessa Armand died of cholera the same year
when the conversation between Clara Zetkin and
Lenin took place. Retrospectively, it is precisely

the letter exchange between Lenin and Inessa that can also provide us with a better understanding of his discussion with Clara Zetkin.

In a letter written to Inessa in January 1915 regarding her plan for a pamphlet on "the demand for freedom of love," Lenin warns her that this demand, in the present social conditions, would "turn out to be a bourgeois, not a proletarian demand", a claim he would repeat to Clara Zetkin five years later. Sexuality for Lenin was *not* a Marxist subject: Inessa's interpretation of "free love" was for him a bourgeois concept and not a proletarian one. What mattered was the objective, class relations, and not subjective wishes.

Trying to understand Inessa's concept of "free love," Lenin enumerates ten possible interpretations:

1. Freedom *from* material (financial) calculations in affairs of love?
2. The same, *from* material worries?
3. From religious prejudices?
4. From prohibitions by Papa, etc.?
5. From the prejudices of "society"?
6. From the narrow circumstances of one's

environment (peasant or petty-bourgeois or bourgeois intellectual)?

7. From the fetters of the law, the courts and the police?
8. From the serious element in love?
9. From child-birth?
10. Freedom of adultery?[14]

Points 1–7 are in his opinion a characteristic of proletarian women, and 8–10 of bourgeois women. "Freedom of love" does not express the idea of "freedom of love" through points 1–7; on the contrary, the readers of the pamphlet would inevitably understand by "freedom of love" something like points 8–10. Inessa defended her work angrily, by saying that even a "fleeting passion" was more poetic and cleaner than "kisses without love." Lenin in turn used her own words and replied:

Kisses without love between a vulgar couple are *dirty*. I agree. To them one should contrast . . . what? . . . One would think: kisses *with* love? While you contrast them with "fleeting" (why fleeting?) "passion" (why not love?) – so, logically, it turns out that kisses without Love (fleeting) are con-

trasted with kisses without love by married people
. . . Strange.[15]

In other words, Lenin agreed that loveless marital
kisses were "dirty." But he couldn't understand
why she posed as an opposition a "fleeting passion": loveless kisses were loveless kisses, be it
a marital or an extramarital affair. As we can
see, there is much more in Lenin's point than a
simple dismissal of "free love" as promiscuity and
adultery. He himself wasn't a loveless kisser, as
Inessa knew very well, and his request for more
self-control and self-discipline even in affairs of
love cannot be understood only as some sort of
"conservatism." Deep in his heart, Lenin was a
romantic. And this is the reason why for him
sexual desire can't be as simple and unimportant
as drinking a glass of water.

Obviously, what he didn't understand was that
Kollontai and Inessa Armand were not aiming at
adultery or promiscuity when demanding "free
love," but at such forms of a relationship in which
neither sex would come without love (one-night
stands, extramarital affairs, etc.), nor love without sex (marital relationships transformed into
habit, etc.). In fact, Lenin and the most radical

reformers of love relationships (Kollontai, Clara Zetkin, etc.) during the early October Revolution had much more in common than they themselves were aware of. The only (albeit a very large one) difference was that Alexandra Kollontai and Inessa Armand were right to develop the idea that the communist revolution has to come hand in hand with a sexual/love revolution, and Lenin, on the contrary, thought it was still not the right time and we had to do the revolution (securing the power) first, and then we could deal with the question of love. For a revolution to succeed, you must take so much care of the most intimate details of the lives of those who are doing the revolution; these two things just can't be treated separately. Even at the very beginning of every revolution, or upheaval, or protest, or occupation, you must deal with the "human factor" (to organize things, channel energy, etc.); you can't ignore desires or libidinal investments. Maybe, communists are really, as Stalin famously said on the occasion of Lenin's death, "people of a special mould," but even people that are made of a special stuff have desires.

Take Lenin. Wasn't he, during his pre-revolutionary period (his emigration to Western

Europe years before the First World War), a skilled hunter in Siberia, chess player, hiker in the Alps, cyclist in the cities of Western Europe? Isn't this "non-geometric Lenin" the true radicality of Lenin as such? On the one hand, commitment to the revolution; on the other, to desire. To love. These are the true "people of a special mould," not Stalin's one. This raises a number of truly traumatic questions: how does Revolution, that is Love, turn into the love of Terror, into terror as love?; how does the need to protect your child transform into violence worthy of every beast that protects its cub?; how does "freedom of love" turn into a nightmare of trying to possess the Other?; how does an openness to a New World sink into the lowest of human passions of assimilating, closure?

One of the possible hermeneutic procedures to trace this transformation maybe lies in detecting the slow, almost invisible transgression, regression, developments during the Revolution. As Nikolai Valentinov, one of Lenin's former colleagues from his exile years in Geneva, recounted in his memoirs *My Encounters with Lenin*, during the early days even before the Revolution, there occurred a serious debate around the question whether a professional revolutionary could legitimately like flowers? "One of Lenin's comrades, animated by a zeal that even his leader judged excessive, claimed it was forbidden: you start by liking flowers and before you know it you are seized by the desire to live like a landowner lazily stretched out in a hammock who reads French novels and is waited on by obsequious valets in the midst of his magnificent garden."[16]

One step further in this hermeneutic investigation would be to trace and collect such seemingly naïve debates on such seemingly banal questions as flowers. It would be a tremendous undertaking to make a sort of ethnography of Revolution: what about alcohol, miniskirts, music, dance, food, books, fashion, etc.? And precisely these fields, which are the most human of all and thus most ideological of all, could reveal how a revolution can easily turn into a regression: when it tends to prohibit, to prescribe, when it occupies the position of the "subject supposed to know."

When the "non-geometric Lenin" turns into "the geometric Lenin" dangers appear. Not when the libidinal energy invested into hiking or cycling threatens the revolution, so that it has – together with sexual energy or Love – to be suppressed, but conversely: when the revolution threatens to swallow this very spontaneity.

The best illustration of this eternal tension between discipline and spontaneity is embodied in Maxim Gorky's well-known anecdote about Lenin listening to Beethoven's sonatas at his home in Moscow in 1920. It provides us with the "missing link" to decipher the profound relationship and letter exchange between Lenin and Inessa Armand. Listening to Beethoven's *Appassionata* played by the Russian Jewish pianist and composer Issay Dobrowen, Lenin famously remarked:

> I know nothing that is greater than the Appassionata: I am ready to listen to it every day. It is amazing, more than human, music. I want to say gentle stupidities and stroke the heads of people who, living in this dirty hell, can create such beauty. But today you must not stroke the head of anyone – they will bite your hand. It is necessary to beat them over the head, beat without mercy, even though in our ideal we are against the use of force against people. Hm-hm, duty is hellishly hard![17]

What if it is precisely this passage that reveals Lenin's secret – his fear of love? What if the

Appassionata stands not only for the "terrible beauty" of the music but for Inessa herself: what if it is an antonomasia – the substitution for love? Possible proof: Angelica Balabanoff, who after keeping a long silence regarding this ticklish subject, observed that Lenin "deeply loved music, and this Krupskaia could not give him. Inessa played beautifully – his beloved Beethoven and other pieces."[18] If we take into account that the year when Lenin visited Gorky was the same year when Inessa died (1920), is it so difficult to imagine a completely devastated and depressed man who was desperate to hear his beloved *Appassionata* again, although his beloved mistress is not playing it anymore, and never will?

As Balabanoff recalls, when Inessa died, he begged her to speak at her funeral because he was utterly broken by her death. At the last moment it was none other than Alexandra Kollontai who arrived and delivered a moving address while "Lenin was plunged in despair, his cap down over his eyes; small as he was, he seemed to shrink and grow smaller. He looked pitiful and broken in spirit."[19] Kollontai recalls: "When her body was brought from the Caucasus and we accompanied her to the cemetery, Lenin was unrecognizable.

He walked with closed eyes; at every moment we thought he would collapse. He was not able to go on living after Inessa Armand. The death of Inessa hastened the development of the sickness which was to destroy him."[20]

Imagine now Lenin hearing the *Appassionata* at Gorky's apartment again. It must have been hellishly hard.

4

The Temptation of Che Guevara: Love or Revolution?

What we encounter in Lenin's "*Appassionata* dilemma" is something that would haunt another great revolutionary many years later. In his "Message to the Tricontinental" in 1967, Ernesto "Che" Guevara made the (in)famous remark about,

> hatred as an element of the struggle, a relentless hatred of the enemy, impelling us over and beyond the natural limitations that man is heir to and transforming him into an effective, violent, selective, and cold killing machine. Our soldiers must be thus; a people without hatred cannot vanquish a brutal enemy.[1]

How are we to evaluate this controversial state-ment if we compare it to the equally famous – and seemingly contrary and contradictory – paragraph from his "Socialism and Man in Cuba" written only two years before, during his three-month trip to Africa:

> At the risk of seeming ridiculous, let me say that the true revolutionary is guided by great feelings of love. It is impossible to think of a genuine revo-lutionary lacking this quality. Perhaps it is one of the great dramas of the leader that he or she must combine a passionate spirit with a cold intelligence and make painful decisions without flinching. Our vanguard revolutionaries must idealize this love of the people, of the most sacred causes, and make it one and indivisible. They cannot descend, with small doses of daily affection, to the level where ordinary people put their love into practice.[2]

On the one hand we have Guevara who is pas-sionately preaching hatred as the crucial fuel of struggle, envisioning revolutionaries as cold kill-ing machines; on the other hand stands a man who is, at the risk of sounding ridiculous, teach-ing that a true revolutionary has to be guided by great feelings of love. How are we to reconcile these two apparently opposite positions present also in Lenin?

Under the protection of a hypothesis we could say that the true radicality of love – as well as the true radicality of revolution – is to be found in a Hegelian *Aufhebung* that doesn't suppress or erase one or the other presupposition: the true radicality of love is to be found in the radicality of revolution, and the radicality of revolution is to be found in true love.

The lesson of the radicality of love/revolution would then be the following one: we should not think in categories of *either/or* but *and/or*. It would be a mistake to perceive Che Guevara's love/ hatred dilemma as a disjunction or contradiction – we have to reach the point where we can understand it as an *and/or* situation: yes it is possible to love and/or hate at the same time. Love and hate are not necessarily opposites, they can lead to a third instance.

Aleida Guevara, the eldest daughter of four children born to Che Guevara and his second wife, Aleida March, gives the needed dialectical twist: "My father knew how to love, and that was the most beautiful feature of him – his capacity to love. To be a proper revolutionary, you have to be a romantic."[3] In other words, revolution can – and must – be grounded in love.

When in "Socialism and Man in Cuba," just after he said that the true revolutionary is guided by great feelings of love, Che warns that "leaders of the revolution have children just beginning to talk, who are not learning to say 'daddy' and that their wives must be part of the general sacrifice of their lives in order to take the revolution to its destiny," Aleida knows very well what he is talking about. When he left Cuba to foment the revolution in Congo, she was only four and a half years old. When he was executed in Bolivia, she was only 6 years old. The true revolutionary has to be a romantic. Sacrifices included.

When we met in Zagreb in May 2013, I had the opportunity to ask Aleida how often she saw her father. She answered that it was very rare, and when he came to visit the family it was "incognito," in the disguise of "father's friend" so the children would not call him "daddy" (*papa*) and reveal his true identity. In this context it becomes clear that Che is actually writing about himself when he is speaking about the leaders of the revolution who have children who are not learning to say "daddy." And it is a historical cruelty that the code for Che among the army members who captured him in Bolivia was neither more nor less than "Papa."[4] It is as if the love of the father whose children, in order to preserve the revolution, were not allowed to learn to say "daddy," was kidnapped by the enemy's hatred who called him "Papa."

This difficult relationship between children and parents goes in both directions: not only that the revolutionary parent (Che) is deprived of his own love toward his children (he must act as if he has no feelings, constantly suppressing his feelings), but the children – if they are conscious of their (not the father's) revolutionary task – have the same relationship toward their own parents as well (the love has to be sublimated into the revolutionary cause, even if the price is to never see the parents again).

This difficult task is best revealed in Che's famous farewell letter to his parents in 1965 prior to his secret embarkment for Congo:

Dear old folks,
(. . .) Many will call me an adventurer, and that I am – only one of a different sort: one who risks his

skin to prove his truths. It is possible that this may be the end. I don't seek it, but it's within the logical realm of probabilities. If it should be so, I send you a final embrace. I have loved you very much, only I have not known how to express my affection. I am extremely rigid in my actions, and I think that sometimes you did not understand me. It was not easy to understand me. Nevertheless, please believe me today. (. . .)

For you, a big hug from your obstinate and prodigal son, Ernesto[5]

His mother, Celia de la Serna, never had the opportunity to read this letter. By the time it arrived in Buenos Aires, she had already died of breast cancer. Although she asked to see him shortly before his departure, Che explained the advanced state of the preparations for his trip had already made this impossible. At the same time, she was hiding the fact that she was terminally ill. Che received the news about his mother's death when he was in Congo and described it as "the saddest news of the whole war."[6] The day he received the news, he wrote a short story titled *La piedra* ("The Stone"), referring to the keychain with a stone that his mother had given him a long time ago. At the beginning of his most intimate confession, he wonders whether it was okay to cry a little and comes to the conclusion that the leader cannot have personal feelings. It's not that he's denied the right to have personal feelings, he simply must not show them like his soldiers might. He then asks himself whether one does not cry because one must not, or because one cannot, and comes to the following conclusion:

> I don't know. I really don't know. I know only that I feel a physical need for my mother to be here so that I can rest my head in her bony lap. I need to hear her call me her 'dear old fella' with such tenderness, to feel her clumsy hand in my hair, caressing me in strokes, like a rag doll, the tenderness streaming from her eyes and voice, the broken channels no longer bearing it to the extremities. Her hands tremble and touch rather than caress, but the tenderness still flows from them. I feel so good, so small, so strong. There is no need to ask her for forgiveness. She understands everything. This is evident in her words 'my dear old fella . . .'[7]

Yes, wives, mothers and children must be part of the general sacrifice of their lives in order to take the revolution to its destiny, but it still doesn't mean the revolutionary is not guided by great feelings of love. Precisely this could be the most accurate definition of true sacrifice: you don't call it sacrifice when you intentionally suppress or abandon something that is of no big value; when you sacrifice something that is of the greatest importance to you and you sacrifice it fully aware of all the consequences without making the quietest sound, then this is real sacrifice. It is the same as a favor: when you give a favor to someone, the moment you start talking about it – mentioning how much you had to sacrifice for it – it fades away, it's not a favor anymore. The same with charity: the only true charity is when you give something to someone in need and don't even allow gratitude – the moment you begin to show off with your charity, it's not charity anymore.

Once Aleida March, Guevara's second wife and the mother of four of his five children, after four decades of chosen silence decided to publish her memoirs, it is precisely this "warm," emotional side of Che that was revealed: he wasn't only a self-described cold killing machine – he was a lover, poet, husband and father of five as well. Her memoirs cover the days when they first met as fellow guerrillas to the moment when she learned of Che's assassination in Bolivia less than a decade later. It is marked by the same *fort-da* destiny of someone who, on the one hand, had deep feelings for his beloved ones, and on the other, suppressed them for the revolutionary cause.

The whole relationship between Aleida March and Che Guevara was a fatal path that wavered between the most passionate feelings and the uttermost fidelity to the revolutionary cause. In a letter from Paris in 1965, Che admits to his wife that he loves her more and more each day and that his home (the children and "the little world" that he can only sense rather than experience) beckons him, but he admits this might be dangerous – it could divert him from his duty. As Aleida herself describes figuratively, "we have became machines focused almost exclusively on combat."[8] On the other hand, echoing Che's own oscillation between hate ("hatred as an element of the struggle") and love ("the true revolutionary is guided by a great feeling of love"), Aleida comes to the same conclusion as her daughter and says Che's commitment "was based on love."[9]

And not only that, but much more than that: Che's revolutionary commitment wasn't only based on love, he was a love machine. Before his trip to Congo, he left his wife an envelope simply addressed "Only for you," containing tape recordings of him reading some of the poems they had shared in their intimate moments. By leaving the tapes, he wrote that he was leaving the best part of himself: it was Che reciting "their poems" such as Pablo Neruda's "Adios: Veinte poemas del amor" or "La sangre numerosa."

When he went to Congo to follow his revolutionary cause, the couple once again went through the difficult times of separation. However, Che – instead of falling under the influence of pathetic passions – wrote a letter to Aleida that if she comes to join him she can't come as his "little wife," but rather as a combatant. In another letter he gives the best possible explanation of what revolutionary love could mean:

> A good part of my life has been like that: having to hold back the love I feel for other considerations. That's why I might be regarded as a mechanical monster. Help me now Aleida, be strong, and don't create problems that can't be resolved. When

we married, you knew who I was. You must do your part so that the road is easier; there is still a long road ahead.

Love me passionately, but with understanding; my path is laid out and nothing but death will stop me. Don't feel sad for me; grab hold of life and make the best of it. Some journeys we will be able to take together. What drives me has nothing to do with a casual thirst for adventures and what that entails. I know that, and so should you. (. . .)[10]

This is not only to be understood as the advice of a radical revolutionary to his wife. It finally brings us closer to the possible definition of the radicality of love as such. The radicality of love does not consist, as it is routinely considered, in the exclusive orientation of one being toward the other: in the fatal erasing of the rest of the world. Love for only one person is a piece of barbarism, as Nietzsche knew very well in *Beyond Good and Evil*, for it is practiced at the expense of all others. However, what is often forgotten is the addition Nietzsche gives to this aphorism: Love of God likewise. And doesn't the same hold for revolution as well? If the revolution is our God, although it can be proclaimed as the most humanist ideal, it can be practiced at the expense of all others (gulag, etc.). What is needed, in order to achieve a truly radical revolution, is love. Because love is, as Alain Badiou puts it, a form of "minimal communism." Love is communism for two. But love is as difficult as communism, and can often end up as tragic as communism. Like revolution, true love is the creation of a new world.[11]

Of course, to achieve this is not easy at all. In another letter, written in Tanzania on November 28, 1965, after the struggle in Congo took an unexpected turn, Che once again expresses this permanent rupture between love and revolution:

> You know I'm a combination of adventurer and bourgeois, with a terrible yearning to come home, while at the same time, anxious to realize my dreams. When I was in my bureaucratic cave, I dreamed of doing what I have begun to do. Now, and for the rest of my journey, I will dream of you, while the children inevitably grow up. They must have such a strange vision of me. How difficult it will be for them one day to love me like a father and not regard me as some distant monster they are obliged to love. (. . .) Now that I am a prisoner, with no enemies nearby, or injustices in my sights,

my need for you is virulent and physiological, and cannot always be calmed by Karl Marx or Vladimir Ilyich.[12]

In February 1966 the time had finally come for a secret reunion of the couple. Che was waiting for her in Tanzania, transformed into another character she almost didn't recognize; he was clean shaven, not wearing the olive green uniform he always wore in Cuba, and she was disguised as well, wearing a black wig and glasses that made her look much older. They would spend the next month in a single, not particularly comfortable room and, according to Aleida, that was one of the happiest times they spent together. During this time in Tanzania, Che recorded himself reading stories for the children and had written his famous farewell letter to Fidel. The reunion would be the first and last time the two spent considerable time alone, without their children or bodyguards; it was as if they finally were on the honeymoon they never had. Nevertheless, following the call of revolution, Che soon left for Prague, and eventually, for Bolivia. In the meantime, Aleida returned to Cuba. A few days later, he sent her a small intimate notebook where in a dark but utterly romantic confession he contemplates the past that has come to an end, and suggests to her: "Don't call me, because I won't be able to hear you. But I will sense you on sunny days, under the renewed caress of bullets."[13]

Here we go again: after the short romantic and passionate reunion, Che is *again* turning into the cold killing machine. But is it really so easy: was he an incurable romantic *or* was he a cold killing machine?

A space for a possible answer opened up in the form of two recent movies that tried to grasp these two aspects of his life that are usually perceived as opposed or even conflicting parts of his personality – Che "before" and "during"/"after" the revolution.

The first is *The Motorcycle Diaries* (2004, Walter Salles), based on Che's diaries about his motorcycle trip throughout South America (14,000 kilometers in just four and a half months), with Mexican actor Gael García Bernal as the 23-year-old Ernesto Guevara, who, with his innocent and tender face, perfectly embodies the younger Che who was still an uncompromising adventurer and more akin to Jack Kerouac than to Lenin.

The other one is *Che* (2008, Steven Soderbergh), based on Guevara's *Reminiscences of the Cuban Revolutionary War* and *Bolivian Diary*, with Benicio Del Toro as the uncompromising revolutionary, who is much more closer to the emotionless killing machine. It is interesting to note that it is not just the content or actor's personifications that clearly show this division (love machine vs. killing machine), but even the filming techniques. For example, in *The Motorcycle Diaries*, close-ups are here to build a more human figure out of the young Che (García Bernal is the ideal face for such a task), while in Soderbergh's *Che*, close-ups of Benicio Del Toro are consciously avoided due to Guevara's belief in collectivism, as Soderbergh himself explained: "You can't make a movie about a guy who has these hard-core sort of egalitarian socialist principles and then isolate him with close-ups."[14]

But it would be wrong to see these as two separate parts of his life. We should rather see it as a logical progression; not as a rupture (the young and innocent adventurer *turned suddenly* into the cold killing machine), but as a continuity and coexistence of both aspects, from the very beginning: it is in revolution where personal characteristics and someone's capability to love can come to their highest expression, and it is in love (when someone, for example, has fanatically fallen in love) when one's aspiration comes to its most dangerous test.

In short: if revolution asks for sacrifices, so does love. But if it is true love, then the sacrifice is not perceived as sacrifice. And if it is a real revolution: any sacrifice, even one's own life, is not perceived as sacrifice. Love *and* revolution can invent moments or unbelievable acts that can be seen as pure madness. But here we should hear Nietzsche again: "There is always some madness in love. But there is also always some reason in madness."[15]

I will always remember a preparatory meeting for the World Social Forum in Monastir, Tunisia in 2012 when, after hours and hours of difficult discussion that seemed to be not productive at all, an activist participant asked Vinod Raina, an Indian activist and comrade who died of cancer in September 2013, "But why are you doing all of these, paying your own flight tickets, coming to Tunisia, having all these boring meetings, hours and hours of discussions, etc.?" Vinod answered: "Because we are mad." I would add today, in remembrance of Vinod: it would be mad not to be mad today.

Thanks to Aleida's memoirs, the world in which we can immerse ourselves is precisely the world of a combination between reason and madness: on the one hand, the commitment of a revolutionary (who would go to Congo after Cuba, and then to Bolivia after Congo, just because he was following the pure Reason of the revolutionary path); on the other hand, a world of constant disguise and drift, a permanent and deadly *fort-da* game under the shadow of the revolution: chasing short moments of reunion, hiding in "safe houses," saying goodbye and farewell kisses, never knowing whether they will meet again. Both are reasonable, both are madness. But true madness would be not doing it, again, and again.

Shorty after Tanzania, one of the happiest times they spent together, they did meet again, this time in Prague. And although they had to maintain strict discipline, functioning in absolute secrecy, "it was enough for us to simply be together again."[16] A few days before Che's final departure for Bolivia, a new separation that would not end with a new reunion, they met in a safe house in Havana together with their children, and Che was already transformed into "Ramón." Aleida introduced the children to a man he said was an Uruguayan friend of their father and who wanted to meet them, because he feared that the older children might tell someone if they recognized him. It was the hardest test they would undergo before never seeing each other again. Che died under the renewed caress of bullets.

5

"What Do I Care about Vietnam, if I Have Orgasm Problems?"

This is the price of revolution. And the sacrifice revolutionaries make is a conscious one; it is an installment paid on the freedom that they are building. The same holds for Lenin and his conscious withdrawal from *Appassionata*/Inessa because of the revolution. If anything, it is obvious that this deadlock can not be resolved by choosing one way or the other, but by combining them: maybe it is possible to stroke the heads of people who, living in this dirty hell, can create such beauty, and at the same time to beat them over the head without mercy. Maybe it is possible to be a husband, lover, poet and revolutionary at the same time.

Unlike Lenin, Che Guevara was pretty close to

achieving this reconciliation of love and revolution. His lesson is the following one: love doesn't necessarily threaten revolution, on the contrary: if we suppress love too much we might easily end up like the October or Iranian Revolution. Yes, we might say: but wasn't Che constantly deprived of the time with his beloved ones (wife, mother, children), wasn't that the price of his revolutionary commitment? Here we should follow Che's own writings and the memories of the ones who loved him and who were not resentful of his almost religious devotion to the revolutionary cause. The solution is not love *or* revolution, but love *and* revolution.

It was already in the year following Che's death, during the worldwide protests of 1968, that this thesis would go through one of its most serious tests. Or as a typical question from these times, attributed to the German political activist Dieter Kunzelmann, put it: "*Was geht mich der Vietnamkrieg an, solange ich Orgasmusschwierigkeiten habe?*" ("What do I care about Vietnam, if I have orgasm problems?"). Instead of the primacy of revolution or love, advocated by Che or Lenin, now the revolutionary subject proclaimed the primacy of sex. There was no revolution without a sexual revolution. It was as if, but mostly without any reference to Alexandra Kollontai and all the discussions that were vibrant during the October Revolution, the same problem of "free love" was on the table again.

The same dilemma between "free love" and "conventional love" – love or revolution – was present during the years of '68 in Germany in the *Kommune 1*. The commune was part of the more radical left wing of the student movement, from which *Die Rote Armee Fraktion* (RAF) developed, and even some later members of the RAF were previously members of the commune. On the one hand, they were influenced by Herbert Marcuse and his theory of the one-dimensional society; on the other hand, it was of course Wilhelm Reich. Microrebellion, with its experiments with drugs and promiscuity, was the word of the day.

One part of this group of young people established a commune in a shared flat at the beginning of 1967 and named it *Kommune 1*. They perceived the nuclear family as the smallest cell of the state from whose oppressive character all institutions (even fascism) are derived; the relationship between men and women as a dependency that disabled their free development as people; private ownership as something that has to be abolished, etc.

Already at the end of 1966, one of the later "patriarchs" of the commune, Dieter Kunzelmann, published a manifesto on establishing revolutionary communes in modern metropolises (*Notizen zur Gründung revolutionärer Kommunen in den Metropolen*), in which he outlines the purpose of the communes. The main purpose of the commune is the "*Aufhebung*" of all "bourgeois dependency relationships (marriage, ownership claims on man, woman and children, etc.)" and the "destruction of the private sphere and all our performed normalities."[1] It is a revolutionary step from the "abstract" struggle to the "concrete" struggle. Instead of a theoretical framework, what counts is "praxis": it is not the class consciousness that leads to praxis, but the other way around – it is praxis that leads to class consciousness. No wonder, then, that the *Kommune 1*, like other similar experiments, would practice various drug experiments, all sorts of different sexual practices, etc.

Kunzelmann is here referring to Marcuse's seminal "Repressive Tolerance" essay from 1965 claiming that our relationship to Praxis and direct action should be characterized by Marcuse's statement that "there is a natural right of resistance for oppressed and overpowered minorities to use extralegal means if the legal ones have proved to be inadequate" (*Repressive Toleranz*). And those, who practice this right of resistance, that goes up to the overthrow (*Umsturz*), do it "because they want to be Men," who no longer accept the rules of a society of total administration and do not "refrain from the outset to counter-violence." Only by "other forms of action" (*Korsch, Vorwort von Gerlach*) can we be true to Che Guevara's statement: "It is the man of the 21st century, that we need to create . . ."[2]

After reading this passage, the only proper historical materialist reaction would be the following one: yes, unintentionally you did create the man of the twenty-first century. It is the man whose "natural right" of resistance turned into the "natural right" of lifestyle. This potential was actually present in the *Kommune 1* from the very beginning: it is the *homo ludens* and not the serious revolutionary subject that was the main proponent of this movement; it was the *Spaßguerilla* ("fun guerrilla") led by Fritz Teufel and not the *Stadtguerilla* ("urban guerrilla") of Rudi Dutschke that served as the background for the commune. It was precisely this mockery of the establishment (the "Pudding Assassination" of US Vice-President Hubert Humphrey; the controversial "Burn, Ware-House, burn!" flyer after the large Brussels department store claimed the lives of over 300 shoppers in 1967, etc.) that led to terrorism (Andreas Baader and Gudrun Ensslin participating in the *Spaßguerilla* performance at Paul Löbe's satirical funeral ceremony, etc.); but on the other hand, it was this very "subversion" that was later co-opted by the establishment and turned into a commodity.

Just several months after the founding of *Kommune 1*, Rudi Dutschke, who had been invited to join them but never did, predicted the possible outcome. In an interview for *Der Spiegel*, Dutschke echoed Lenin's words: "The exchange of women and men is nothing else but the implementation of the bourgeois exchange principle under pseudorevolutionary auspices."[3] That truly "free love" is not such an easy praxis as the communards first thought, became clear at the peak of *Kommune 1*. In 1969, Jimi Hendrix came to Berlin for a concert and paid a short visit to the commune. Soon Uschi Obermaier – known also as "the most beautiful face of '68" – ended up with him in his hotel. The reaction of the communards was embodied in the angry reaction by Kunzelmann who screamed at them: "Did you have a good fuck in the Hotel? Are you afraid of spectators? Why don't you do it here? We want to see you fuck. We want to see you fuck here!"[4]

When Uschi Obermeier first came to the Commune, after escaping the life of her conservative parents in Munich, the communards gave her the books of Mao and Marx as a sort of initiation – recall Godard's brilliant anticipation of events to come in *La Chinoise* (filmed just one year before '68) – but she thought the words were "too unattractive."[5] It is a supreme irony that Uschi Obermeier was first seen as an intruder and outsider, but it was she who made *Kommune 1* so popular. Not because she slept with Mick Jagger and Keith Richards, among others, but because the politicization of the private sphere literally became more attractive than the "too unattractive" politicized words. When she first arrived at the commune, she immediately fell in love with Rainer Langhans, but couldn't stand his open sexual relationship with other women.

Nevertheless, soon she became a bigger communard than the communards themselves, remembered to be saying: "Only when you hate someone, you can prohibit him something what makes him joy. When I love someone, then I am happy because of everything that makes him happy. If he sleeps with someone else, I am not deprived of anything."[6]

In the movie based on her memoirs, *Das Wilde Leben* (Eight Miles High, 2007, Achim Bornhak), there is a wonderful scene when the members of the Commune, after a violent protest, sit in their apartment the next morning and check the newspapers (*Stern*, *Der Spiegel*, etc.). On every cover there was the photo of Uschi Obermeier. One of the members starts criticizing it, but then Langhans says they should use the capitalist motto "sex sells" for their own struggle. In the end, it was Uschi Obermeier who became the most emblematic face of the Commune.

Soon he and Uschi got an invitation to meet the Rolling Stones in London. Langhans soon sank into jealousy, despite the fact that he was preaching "free love" when Uschi was jealous. Kunzelmann soon became addicted to heroin and was expelled from the commune (like many others before him). This was the beginning of the end of *Kommune 1*. It was the victim of its own ideology. In the end it was Rudi Dutschke who was proven right when he answered a seemingly stupid question by a *Der Spiegel* journalist, whether the "Horror-Kommune" isn't "only a club of high-grade neurotics":

It is that as well, but it is not the Commune to blame, but the society, which made the conditions for such human deformities. The image of the naked Commune members, that was published by *Der Spiegel* – but with erased genitals, which says something about *Der Spiegel* – seems to me to be an adequate expression of the current situation of the Commune. The picture reproduces the gas chamber milieu of the Third Reich; for behind this exhibitionism hides a helplessness, fear and horror. The Commune members see themselves as oppressed and marginalized members of this society.[7]

Who could tell at that time (it was 1967 when Dutschke uttered these prophetic words) that one of the subjects of another cult photo – the one from *Stern* from 1969 with naked Uschi

Obermeier in the foreground – would soon become one of the leading members of the RAF? It was Holger Meins, the cult figure of "Germany in Autumn," who was captured together with Andreas Baader and Jan-Carl Raspe in June 1972. In prison, Meins and the other RAF prisoners launched several hunger strikes against the terrrible conditions of their imprisonment. Meins died by starvation in November 1974. His death sparked many protests across Europe and further terrorist acts – among them, the Embassy siege in Stockholm in 1975, by terrorists who named their group after him – "Holger Meins Kommando." Following his death caused by his hunger strike in Stammheim, Meins became some sort of "martyr" of the revolution, and the last known photo was a sad, self-fulfilling prophecy of Dutschke's words: weighing only 39 kilos at the age of 33, the former member of the Commune really looked like a victim of Auschwitz. In the end it was Dutschke, with his raised fist at the open grave of Holger Meins, who uttered the prophetic words: *Der Kampf geht weiter*!

Unlike other member of the Commune, what Meins understood very well is that the human body isn't only a terrain for sexual liberation, various sorts of "free sex" experiments, etc. He went much further than that. Only six months before his death, he wrote a letter in prison under the title *Die Waffe Mensch* ("The man as weapon"), where he says that "we are imprisoned, but we are not disarmed (. . .) We have two powerful weapons: our brains and our life, our consciousness and our being."[8] This was his announcement for the longest and most difficult of the collective hunger strikes of the RAF prisoners. The intention of Meins' words becomes even clearer when we read his letter of June 5, 1974, in which he says: "The Price sisters, they live 10 × 10 × 10,000 years!"[9] It means: it is precisely through the hunger strike that one can achieve eternity. The so-called "Price sisters" were jailed for being part of the IRA and conducted a hunger strike that lasted over 200 days.

As we know, the hunger strike, as a form of non-violent resistance or political means of pressure, has a long history: from pre-Christian Ireland to the ancient practice of hunger strikes in India, when protesters – typically indebted people – would come to the door of an offending party and go on hunger strike. The most famous example is, of course, Mahatma Gandhi, who was protesting British colonial rule of India in his several famous hunger strikes. Then there were also the British and American suffragettes, etc.

The most notable examples are, of course, the Irish republicans, and it brings us back to Holger Meins' thesis that the human body can serve as a weapon. Just after the end of the Irish Civil War, in 1923, more than 8,000 IRA prisoners went on hunger strike, then again in the 1940s, and again in the 1970s.

In fact, it was precisely the IRA hunger strikes that were, among other things, an inspiration for the RAF hunger strikes a few years later. The conditions of the RAF prisoners in Stammheim were a Guantanamo *avant la lettre*: all prisoners were put in solitary confinement, the lights were left on day and night, it was complete isolation.

To this day the best description was given by none other than Ulrike Meinhof:

> The feeling, one's head explodes (the feeling, the top of the skull will simply split, burst open) –
> the feeling, one's spinal column presses into one's brain
> the feeling, one's brain gradually shrivels up like dried fruit, for example –

the feeling, one is constantly, imperceptibly, flooded, one is remote-controlled –

the feeling, one's associations are hacked away –

the feeling, one pisses the soul out of one's body, like when one cannot hold water –

the feeling, the cell moves. One wakes up, opens one's eyes: the cell moves; afternoon, if the sun shines in, it is suddenly still. One cannot get rid of the feeling of motion. One cannot tell whether one shivers from fever or from cold –

one cannot tell why one shivers – one freezes.

. . .

The feeling of traveling through space packed into a barrel so that the acceleration causes your skin to flatten –

Kafka's penal colony – The version with a bed of nails –

A non-stop rollercoaster ride.[10]

Isn't this one of the best descriptions of what happens to the human body and mind when one is in prison? Moreover, what all these examples show – the hunger strike of Holger Meins and the feeling of Ulrike Meinhof – is what in political theory, from Foucault to Agamben, is called biopolitics. But the *homo sacer* can strike back

– the prisoners themselves used the human body as their last resort, as their last means and last terrain of struggle.

Let's take an example from the IRA again. In 1978 prisoners started something that would be known as the so-called "dirty protest." They refused to leave their cells to shower or use the lavatory, and the prison officers were unable to clean them. It was a clear shift in power dynamics. Instead of being pure body objects, the women decorated the cells with menstrual blood; their bodies were now political weapons. The body was transformed into a site of resistance, rather than an object of discipline and normalization.

If you live under the conditions of biopolitics, if you are deprived of everything and your body is the object of discipline and punish, then the last resort is precisely the body. Or take another, older, notable example – that of the Marquis de Sade. We know that he spent 32 years of his life imprisoned. But what is less known is that at one point prison guards confiscated every piece of writing material they could from his prison, and it is said that he would then take sharp objects and start carving his writings into the walls, and when that was taken from him, he would bite into his fingers and write in blood. . .

What we see in Ulrike Meinhof's statement and the Marquis de Sade's practice is the following: under those conditions, there is no difference between the body and the mind – the mind becomes the body and the body turns into one's mind. It is not only a reversal of the standard Platonic-Christian positive valuation of the mind over the body. The point is not so simple as to say that now the body has a primacy over the mind. What becomes evident in "The man as weapon" is a tendency to overcome the dualistic opposition between body and mind itself. That is the reason why Nietzsche never speaks about *Körper*, but about *Leib*. *Körper* would be a mortal body, and *Leib* is much more than only a body, it's a unity of body, mind, and soul.

And it is exactly here that we should return to the beginning. The "radical" examples used – RAF hunger strikes, IRA dirty protest, and not to mention suicide as the ultimate weapon – show that the body isn't always a political object, but can also be a political subject. The recent protests in Turkey gave us at least two confirmations that the "body can be a weapon."

The first was a dance protest in solidarity with demonstrators occupying Gezi Park in Istanbul held by members of Turkey's State Opera and Ballet. One of the protesters said that dancing on stage was the only way they could express themselves: "Our only aim, as we can only express ourselves by dancing, is to show our protest like this too." The other example is the so-called, now famous, "Standing Man." Does it come as a surprise that this man wasn't a simple protester? His name is Erdem Gunduz and he is a dancer and choreographer. The first evening he was standing there for five hours and staring at a portrait of Mustafa Kemal Ataturk. Soon, similar protests consisting of simply stopping and standing still spread everywhere in Turkey.

It was a brilliant strategy, reminiscent of Tiananmen Square's "Tank Man" or the recent silent standing performance by Jelena Topić from Bosnia. Why is it a good strategy? Because nonviolence is much harder to deal with than violent protest, the government now was tempted to arrest people who were doing nothing more than standing still. Of course, they arrested the standing people in the end as well.

What the members of Turkey's State Opera

and Ballet and Erdem Gunduz repeated is the famous slogan of the New Dance Group, a working-class organization for dance, formed in New York in 1932 by two Jewish dance students, which states: "Dance is a weapon in the class struggle."

The main concept of the New Dance Group is what an ideal dance group should look like. Besides dancers, it attracted ordinary workers as well. And just for a dime, the students would receive an hour-long dance class, an hour of improvisation based on a social theme, and an hour of discussion on social issues. As we know, in 1932, 11 workers' dance groups in New York joined together into the Workers' Dance League. That's exactly what we need today: a Workers' Dance League. Or at least, dancers who are aware dancing is not always "pure art," it is always a political act as well.

And here we return to the problem of sex. As long as it is perceived as a means in itself, not as a weapon in the class struggle, but as the last pleasant destination, it is not at all revolutionary. Andreas Baader was fully right in his unforgettable saying *Ficken und Schießen ist ein Ding* ("Fucking and shooting are the same thing"), but the real problem appears when fucking becomes more important than shooting. And the other way around as well: when only shooting becomes important.

A perfect example of another group, besides *Kommune 1*, in which fucking became more important than shooting is the American version of the RAF – it is, of course, the Weather Underground. The US anti-Vietnam War movement soon took the same direction as the German '68 movement, not only bombs and violence, but also "sexual liberation." After the Weather Underground members had rejected non-violence as a viable tactic, they moved into collective houses in order to "smash monogamy" as well – exclusive relationships between men and women were now seen as reinforcing the old patterns of female subservience. It is best described by Mark Rudd, former 1960s radical student leader and fugitive member of the Weather Underground. One way to "smash monogamy" consisted in

> extreme sexual experiences. Group sex, homosexuality, and casual sex hook-ups were all tried as we attempted to break out from the repression of the past into the revolutionary future. (. . .) Since sex

was the ultimate intimacy in human relations, we were building political collectives bonded with this intimacy among all members, not between monogamous couples.[11]

But this had a peculiar price. As another member of the Weather Underground, Bill Ayers, recalls in his memoirs *Fugitive Days*, "smashing monogamy took a lot of energy – it was part of the political line to renounce all the habits and cultural constraints of the past, to make ourselves into selfless tools of struggle. We were an anti-Puritan police force – you were supposed to fuck, no matter what."[12]

And, OK, this might still sound subversive, but the true problem of this "sexual liberation" can be found in other parts of Mark Rudd's memoirs. Just take the following one:

For me it meant freedom to approach any woman in any collective. And I was rarely turned down, such was the aura and power of my leadership position. For the second time in my life, my fantasies were being fulfilled: I could have almost any of these beautiful, strong revolutionary women I desired.[13]

When was the first time that his fantasies were fulfilled? While he was chairman of Students for a Democratic Society (SDS). In 1968 he led the occupation of five buildings on Columbia's campus to protest the university's funding of the Vietnam War. In many ways, he became the face of student organizing and mass protest. He travelled the country, holding talks at various schools; his picture was featured in the *New York Times* and *Newsweek*; he was a star. And it is from this period that this confession comes:

> I felt no qualms at all about sleeping with whoever was available on the road, even though I had a new girlfriend back in New York. I was a woman junkie. I was fulfilling my longtime sexual fantasy of sleeping with a lot of women. The numbers seemed to prove to me that I was attractive and virile. Sometimes before going to sleep, I'd count the women I'd made love with since I started in high school.[14]

How is this to be read? Of course, Rudd is cynical and auto-ironical, but what all these confessions show is that "smashing monogamy," even if it could have been a subversive act in the beginning, wasn't subversive at all. It only proved to be useful to "woman junkies" like him, who even counted the women he slept with in order to prove his own virility. Rudi Dutschke was right again: the exchange of women and men is nothing else but the application of the bourgeois exchange principle under pseudorevolutionary auspices. And here we turn again to Lenin's critique of the "glass of water theory."

Afterplay: The Radicality of Love

So, after all these versions and perversions of love, can we finally answer what the true Radicality of Love would or could be? As we have seen, revolution gives us some possible indications or even lessons: like the first encounter of a revolutionary moment, one must *fall in love*: there is no love without the fall. On the one side, this fall consists in the incredible moments when you occupy a square or die under the renewed caress of bullets, and on the other, you can be sure you are already in the fall, you are falling, when you suddenly become paralyzed by someone's eyes.

This is the first radical consequence of love: all that you took for granted, the very foundations of your whole daily life, the past and the future, becomes inherently painted by this new present which reconstitutes your past and future. But, still, is this love? No, we should be more precise here: it is the first radical consequence of something that might transform itself into Love. The act of "falling in love" is still not love. It is what the Sufis would call *hawa*. Only when we come to the level of *hubb*, when the dirt sinks to the bottom, can it become something more. But again, a new danger lurks here: it is *'ishq*, when *hubb* blinds the lover's eyes except to the Beloved.

In other words, just after the fall (and it is still part of the "fall") – if it was a real *fall* – comes the obsession with the Beloved, the urge for isolation: it is only me and my Beloved that matters, I don't care for the rest of the world, neither for my mother nor for my friends. One of the best illustrations is to be found in Bertolucci's *Last Tango in Paris* (1972). It is the primordial scene of isolation: Paul (Marlon Brando) and Jeanne (Maria Schneider) are enclosed in an abandoned apartment in which they reject everything that ties them to civilization – names, language and, of course, clothes. And when does this fatal *fall* start to collapse? In the moment when they leave the apartment and Jeanne finally reveals what she wanted to know during the whole passionate affair: Paul recently lost his wife who committed suicide; he is the owner of an obscure hotel, etc. Although their whole relationship was on the verge of sado-masochism in which the main role was taken by Paul (best exemplified in the legendary butter scene with Maria Schneider on the floor), it is he who eventually overcomes the fall and arrives at love.

He comes to Jeanne and says: "It's me again."

Jeanne replies: "It's over."

Paul: "That's right. It's over and then it begins again."

Jeanne: "What begins again? I don't understand anything anymore."

Paul: "There's nothing to understand. We left the apartment, and now we begin and love all the rest of it."

Jeanne: "The rest of it?"

Paul: "Yeah, listen. I'm 45. I'm a widower. I own a little hotel. It's kind of a dump, but not completely a flophouse. Then I used to live on my luck and I got married, and my wife killed herself."

If there ever was a fatal fall, than it is in *Last Tango in Paris*. But what we can see here is that an even bigger space of risk, of openness, of a whole new world and all the dangers it brings along, is opened by the next step after the fall. It is precisely this moment that is overlooked by all the interpretations of Bertolucci's moment. The really shocking moment is not the sado-masochistic love affair as such, the passionate relationship between Marlon Brando and Maria Schneider that went far beyond the movie. No, it is this real traumatic crack opened by leaving the apartment. The first radical test of love appears once you leave the apartment; once the masks are removed and the moment has come to get familiar with all the dirty details (45 years old, widower, owner of a hotel, etc.).

There can only be one outcome of the desire for absolute isolation – if we leave aside fantasy endings like "and they lived happily ever after." It is best portrayed in another masterpiece of twentieth-century cinematography. It is, of course, Liliana Cavani's *Il portiere di notte* (The Night Porter) from 1974. Here we can find out what would happen with Paul and Jeanne if they had continued their game and they never revealed their masks.

It is a story of reunion of a former SS officer

with a concentration camp inmate. Max (Dirk Bogarde) is now a night porter in a Viennese hotel, all the time under the surveillance of his former Nazi colleagues who assume and finally reveal his secret sexual relationship with Lucy (Charlotte Rampling), that had already started in the concentration camp and now, ten years later, finds its final installment. The only way the two of them can continue their relationship consists in hiding in his apartment. Their obsessive love thus again creates a situation peculiar to the concentration camp. Isolation ends in paranoia, and they can't get out of the apartment. Once they exhaust all their food supplies, reduced to what Agamben would call "bare life," starving, with their everyday existence reduced to the animal level, the only way out of this situation becomes an "honorable" death: Max dressed as a SS officer and Lucy as the concentration camp inmate, holding hands and walking across the bridge on which they are eventually killed.

Each isolation consists in the desire to possess another. In this regard the isolation is essentially an impossibility. It is an impossible place and, although the lovers know it, they strive precisely for this very impossibility. As Jean Baudrillard puts it in his *Fatal Strategies* in a beautiful description:

> To love someone is to isolate him from the world, wipe out every trace of him, dispossess him of his shadow, drag him into a murderous future. It is to circle around the other like a dead star and absorb him into a black light. Everything is gambled on an exorbitant demand for the exclusivity of a human being, it may be. This is doubtless what makes it a passion: its object is interiorized as an ideal end, and we know that the only ideal object is a dead one.[1]

The only problem with Baudrillard is that one small, but nonetheless important, detail should be added if we really want to understand the difference between *falling in love* and Love: the demand for the exclusivity of a human being is a characteristic of falling in love, whereas Love is the pure opposite. It is not radical to circle around the other like a dead star and absorb him into a black light. This would be what Michael Hardt calls "love of the same," a unification through erasing differences. It is a narcissistic form of love.

Is the solution then what the generation of '68 – *Kommune 1* or the Weather Underground –

understood as "free love"? Instead of one partner, we have several. We abandon jealousy and individualism to reach the joy of a collective love? If all the above-mentioned (per)versions of this sort of "free love" are still not sufficient to understand that, we must reach far beyond: maybe someone who led a double life with two women and was torn between two relationships could help us. This is Daniel Bensaïd from his memoirs:

> In these years of liberation of morals and attacks on the sanctuarising of private life, militants sought to free themselves from outdated prejudices about relationships and fidelity. Despite solemn shared proclamations of liberation, however, individuals were not all equal in the face of jealousy and heartache. The old Adam (or Eve) is not so easily shed. If one might hope to overthrow political power by assault, or revolutionise property relations by legislative decision, the Oedipus complex or the incest temptation cannot be abolished by decree. The transformation of mentalities and cultures is a matter of very *longue durée*.[2]

Thanks to the published letters of Simone de Beauvoir to Sartre, we can now see that even the immortal heroes of a "transparent" and "open" relationship were not always happy or satisfied with their pact to experience contingent love affairs. Simone de Beauvoir also felt jealousy and she was not so independent of Sartre as it was thought before. It is enough to read her letter from October 26, 1939 to get a sense of it:

As I've already told you, I'm not jealous of your feelings for people. But I am jealous of people's feelings for you (it's not just a theme for a novel!). Wanda doesn't bother me, because in her little consciousness you're such an odd being, so different from the one I love. But Bienenfeld irritates me because it's a more serious version of you, and because she's so restless, and because she theorizes her love for you with such self-importance – it has its own solid violence, moreover. When you're there, I know quite well our love is the truest; but from afar I find it a burden to see you trailing round in other hearts. At the present – as is sometimes the case – I'd so like to be alone with you, without Kosakiewitch, without Bienenfeld, just you and me. I know it's foolish – since if you were there there'd be nothing but you and me, despite all the others – but you're far away. O yourself, I love you so, love you in the real sense of the word. I have a passionate need for you. O little shadow, do become flesh and blood – I so need your little arms around me![3]

As we can see, the transformation of love under revolutionary auspices is no easy task at all. We should conduct the experiment, take Alexandra Kollontai's "Theses on Communist Morality in the Sphere of Marital Relations" (published in 1921) and offer her thesis no. 4 to Simone de Beauvoir: "A jealous and proprietary attitude to the person loved must be replaced by a comradely understanding of the other and an acceptance of his or her freedom. Jealousy is a destructive force of which communist morality cannot approve."[4] And now read Simone de Beauvoir's letter again! Did she really violate and transgress the communist morality because she couldn't watch Sartre's countless affairs anymore? Lenin's critique of the "glass of water theory" wasn't right when it came to the understanding of what "free love" really meant for Kollontai, but on the other hand, it was he who had already predicted Simone de Beauvoir's deadlock. What de Beauvoir and Sartre had was a "communism for two;" they enacted what Kollontai prescribed in her "Theses on Communist Morality" and if we want to see whether it functions in reality, we should look at their specific relationship. Yes, we could say in the end, it did function, but . . . it's not easy at all!

The point, among others, where Kollontai was right (and we must say it was one of the most radical interpretations of love up to today!) was the sphere of property. All her theses on the new love morality were directed against the idea that a couple begins to treat one another in terms of property relations, which goes so far that the lovers sometimes even rush to privatize the heart of the other person's being. This privatization of the most intimate sphere is still something that haunts sexual relationships. Kollontai's concept of "free love," by which she meant sexual relations liberated from bourgeois possessiveness, is of utmost importance for today's understanding of love. What Lenin – as seen in his discussion with Clara Zetkin – obviously didn't understand is that Kollontai saw the outbreak of casual sexual encounters as often exploitative (of women by men for their private sexual benefit) and irresponsible (women left to care for the children in a social context which was still not capable to spare social resources for collective raising of children).

What Kollontai couldn't predict is that the most progressive measures she had conducted (her efforts to nationalize maternity and infant care), as the only woman in the Soviet cabinet and first woman in history who had ever been recognized as a member of a government, would soon turn into the pure opposite, into a dystopian future where love would be abolished. We don't need science fiction stories or movies like the recent *The Giver* (in which no feelings are permitted and children are assigned to families), if we can examine the experiment called Khmer Rouge.

But first, let us take Kollontai's speech to the third all-Russian conference heads of the Regional Women's Departments in 1921 about "Prostitution and ways of fighting it":

The bourgeois world gave its blessing to the exclusiveness and isolation of the married couple from the collective; in the atomized and individualistic bourgeois society, the family was the only protection from the storm of life, a quiet harbour in a sea of hostility and competition. The family was an independent and enclosed collective. In communist society this cannot be. Communist society presupposes such a strong sense of the collective that any possibility of the existence of the isolated, introspective family group is excluded. At the present moment ties of kinship, family and even of married life can be seen to be weakening. New ties between working people are being forged and comradeship, common interests, collective responsibility and faith in the collective are establishing themselves as the highest principles of morality.[5]

Yes, we know very well, especially today, that the atomized and individualized family unit was the perfect prerequisite for the accumulation of capital. Thomas Piketty provided us with empirical and theoretical research on the long-term evolution of wealth and inheritance. But did the communist societies really abolish this trend or was the party *nomenklatura* another version of accumulation by inheritance? If we want to see the final consequence of Kollontai's abolition of families, let us not be scared to look at the Khmer Rouge in Cambodia.

Like Kollontai, the Khmer Rouge – in their

own obscene vision of communism – insisted that the isolated "couple" as a special unit does not answer the interests of communism and that the interests of the individual must be subordinated to the collective. We know very well that the Khmer Rouge, once they officially seized power in 1975, aimed to destroy all personal belongings (glasses, souvenirs, etc.) in order to create the New People. Instead of individuals, they created a society where each member of the collective had to eat together, the only possession allowed was a spoon and everyone had to share everything. And this was still not all: one of the most important fields of the Khmer Rouge revolution was the transformation of the family unit.

Only in recent years, thanks to the Extraordinary Chambers in the Courts of Cambodia (ECCC), have we gained a better insight into the systematic and widespread practice of forced marriages that took place throughout the country in nearly every village. Between 1975 and 1979 at least 250,000 Cambodian women between 15 and 35 years of age were forced into marriages by the ominous Angkar, the faceless and lawless "Organization." Of course, our first spontaneous reaction would be the following: how is that in any way connected to Kollontai's concept of "free love"? Isn't forced marriage the pure opposite of "free love"? Yes, but the nightmare of the Khmer Rouge evolved out of the same idea that the State has to be the only family and that individuals should be part of a collective.

In practice, it looked like this: couples were arbitrarily married, without choice or consent, and even pressured to consummate their marriage in order to ensure the emergence of a next generation of workers (the New People) that would have less family loyalty and be more loyal to the State. By breaking family bonds and taking the decision of whom to marry out of the hands of citizens, it was now the State was regulating even love. "The use of forced marriage in particular was systematic and widespread, employed by the regime to secure loyalty to the Government by breaking family bonds and taking [the] major life decision [of] who to marry out of the hands of citizens and entrusting it to the State."[6]

So where does all this leave us today? In the current neoliberal deadlock in which the "welfare state" is being demolished on a daily level all over the world, including health care and child care, Kollontai's radical reforms of welfare and her unrealized legislative proposals (known under the incorrect name of the "nationalization of women") look like a science fiction story from a different universe. This radical universe included foundling homes, homes for the aged, orphanages, free hospitals for the needy, the pension system in general, the educational system, etc.[7] This still, and especially today, remains a guideline for every radical politics that wants to come close to the name of Communism.

On the other hand, and it is here that we encounter a real problem, if the idea of welfare gets applied to love as well, we might easily end up in something we might call the "nationalization of love." Every progressive state should have such a legislature on marriage, divorce, homosexual relations, etc., like in the early period of the October Revolution, and many states of the twenty-first century, even in the "civilized West," are still centuries away from such progressive reforms. However, as soon as the State starts to intervene in the most intimate spheres of human lives, we might end up in the dystopia of the Khmer Rouge. The lesson of this complex is outlined in the discussion between Lenin and Kollontai. None of the positions, neither Lenin's about suppressing

Revolution = God = Love

emotions (remember the *Appassionata*) nor Kollontai's about the "glass of water," is right or wrong; what is needed is not to choose between the first or the second position, but to create a third one. And it is Che and his love story that provides at least some hints in which direction this third position could go. To be devoted to the Beloved one and the Revolution at the same time is the true Radicality of Love.

There can be three in a relationship, the Lovers (two) and the Third instance (the Revolution). And, unexpectedly, it brings us to the Trinity. For (true) Christianity, love reflects the love of God. God is Love. God is in the foundation of every love. In this God who is love, Christian theology finds the Trinity: Father, Son, and the Holy Spirit who love each other, and this is called *Perichoresis*. It is best illustrated by the Borromean rings or the *Scutum Fidei*, as shown in figure 3.

What we can see here is co(-)inherence, a circumincession in which the relations between Father, Son, and Holy Spirit are non-directional – NON EST. The love between Father, Son, and Holy Spirit is a love without the relation of *complementarity*. Complementarity means mutual

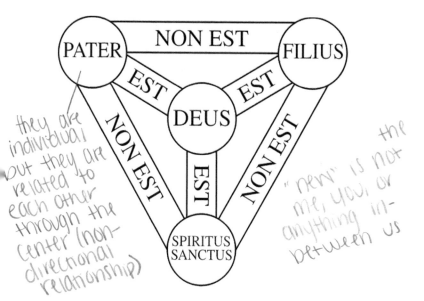

they are individual but they are related to each other through the center (non-directional relationship)

"new" is not me, you, or anything in-between us

Figure 3 Borromean rings or the *Scutum Fidei*

compatibility. In the Christian concept of love, the ideal is not a complementary love. Man and woman are not compatible, but the point is that two people (even man and man, or woman and woman) recognize themselves as the reflection of God, and that they love and respect each other as Father and Son. No one gives what the other does (or doesn't) have; each of them opens up the space for the other and its freedom.[8] Real love is thus the relation of NON EST to the one which is EST. In Christian theology this is God, but why wouldn't we call it Revolution?

Notes

Foreplay: To Fall in Love, or Revolution

1 Søren Kierkegaard, *Works of Love*, Harper Perennial, New York, 2009, pp. 51–2.
2 I rely here on Süleyman Derin's excellent *Love in Sufism. From Rabia to Ibn al-Farid*, Insan Publications, Istanbul, 2008.
3 *Love in Sufism*, p. 199.
4 C. L. R. James, *The Black Jacobins: Toussaint L'Ouverture and the San Domingo Revolution*, Vintage, New York, 1989.
5 The anecdote is retold by the American screenwriter and director Ben Hecht, in his memoirs: Ben Hecht, *A Child of the Century*, Primus, New York, 1985, p. 222.

1. Love in the Age of Cold Intimacies

1 See Eva Illouz, *Cold Intimacies: The Making of Emotional Capitalism*, Polity Press, London, 2007.
2 "Wir fordern die Enteignung Axel Springers – Gespräch mit dem Berliner FU-Studenten Rudi Dutschke (SDS)," *Der Spiegel*, 10 July 1967, p. 32, available online: http://www.spiegel.de/spiegel/print/d-46225038.html
3 www.grindr.com
4 Jamie Woo, *Meet Grindr*, Kindle Edition, 2013.
5 https://www.youtube.com/watch?v=qLblwVUEHyw
6 'Avec Tinder, du sexe et beaucoup de bla-bla', *Le Monde*, 9 August 2014, available online: http://www.lemonde.fr/societe/article/2014/08/09/avec-tinder-du-sexe-et-beaucoup-de-bla-bla_4469392_3224.html?xtmc=tinder&xtcr=1
7 https://www.youtube.com/watch?v=9V_oxDUgoho
8 https://www.youtube.com/watch?v=2C83tbuBmWY
9 https://www.youtube.com/watch?feature=player_embedded&v=lu4ukHmXKFU
10 https://www.youtube.com/watch?feature=player_embedded&v=6oxDsEVqnyY
11 See Franco 'Bifo' Berardi, *Heroes: Mass Murder and Suicide*, Verso, London, 2015.
12 http://www.fastcodesign.com/3028019/anti-social-network-helps-you-avoid-people-you-dont-want-to-see).
13 http://ilovechrisbaker.com/cloak/
14 Charles Nicholl, *Somebody Else: Arthur Rimbaud in Africa 1880–91*, University of Chicago Press, Chicago, IL, 1999, p. 164.

2. Desire in Tehran

1 Gilles Deleuze & Félix Guattari, *Anti-Oedipus. Capitalism and Schizophrenia*, University of Minnesota Press, Minneapolis, MN, 2000, p. 118.

2 David Lloyd Hoffmann, *Stalinist Values: The Cultural Norms of Soviet Modernity, 1917–1941*, Cornell University Press, Ithaca, NY, 2003.

3 Imam Khomeini, *The Position of Women from the Viewpoint of Imam Khomeini*, Institute of Imam Khomeini's Works, 2000, p. 143.

4 For more on the Shah's urbanization changes, see Talinn Grigor, "The king's white walls. Modernism and bourgeois architecture," in B. Devos & C. Werner (eds), *Culture and Cultural Politics Under Reza Shah: The Pahlavi State, New Bourgeoisie and the Creation of a Modern Society in Iran*, Routledge, London, 2014.

5 See Hundertwasser, "Die Fensterdiktatur und das Fensterrecht," January 22, 1990, available online: http://www.hundertwasser.de/deutsch/texte/philo_fensterdiktatur.php

6 See Peter Chelkowski & Hamid Dabashi, *Staging a Revolution: The Art of Persuasion in the Islamic Republic of Iran*. New York University Press, New York, 1999.

7 Khomeini, *The Position of Women*, p. 118.

8 http://rezahakbari.com/2014/01/25/pallet-band-protests-the-ban-of-showing-musicals-instruments-on-iranian-tv-by-miming/

9 Khomeini, *The Position of Women*, p. 125.

10 Simurg Aryan, Homa Aryan, & J. Alex Halderman, "Internet Censorship in Iran: A First Look," in:

Proceedings of the 3rd *USENIX Workshop on Free and Open Communication on the Internet,* August 2013, available online: http://jhalderm.com/pub/papers/iran-foci13.pdf

11 Collin Anderson & Nima Nazeri, "Citation Filtered: Iran's Censorship of Wikipedia," November 2013, available online: http://www.global.asc.upenn.edu/fileLibrary/PDFs/CItation_Filtered_Wikipedia_Report_11_5_2013-2.pdf

12 George Orwell, *Nineteen Eighty-Four,* Signet Classic, London, 1950, p. 68.

13 Blu Tirohl, "We are the dead . . . you are the dead: An Examination of Sexuality as a Weapon of Revolt in Nineteen Eighty-Four," *Journal of Gender Studies,* Volume 9, Issue 1, 2000, pp. 55–56.

14 George Orwell, *Nineteen Eighty-Four,* p. 113.

15 Orwell, *Nineteen Eighty-Four,* p. 133.

16 A term coined by Brian McNair in the book of the same title: *Striptease Culture,* Routledge, London, 2002.

17 http://pando.com/2014/07/15/irans-wildly-mixed-feelings-toward-social-media-continue-as-it-sentences-eight-facebook-users-to-a-combined-127-years-in-prison/

18 http://www.theguardian.com/world/2010/dec/07/wikileaks-cables-saudi-princes-parties

19 http://musicfreedomday.org/wp-content/uploads/2012/02/MusicFreedomReport_Libya_UK.pdf

20 "WikiLeaks Cables Detail Qaddafi Family's Exploits," *The New York Times,* February 22, 2011, available online: http://www.nytimes.com/2011/02/23/world/africa/23cables.html?_r=0

21 http://www.theguardian.com/world/2009/sep/23/gad dafi-tent-ban-bedford-newyork

22 Saif al-Islam Alqadhafi, "The Role of Civil Society in the Democratization of Global Governance Institutions: From 'Soft Power' to Collective Decision-Making?" PhD Thesis, London School of Economics, submitted in September 2007.

23 "'Horrific': David Miliband's furious reaction as it emerges Gaddafi's son gave university lecture in his father's name." *Daily Mail*, 7 March 2011.

24 http://news.bbc.co.uk/2/hi/programmes/from_our_ own_correspondent/4379499.stm

25 https://www.marxists.org/reference/archive/hoxha/wo rks/1965/10/26.htm

26 Pardis Mahdavi, *Passionate Uprisings: Iran's Sexual Revolution*, Stanford University Press, Stanford, CA, 2008, p. 57.

27 I owe this point to Tonči Valentić (Croatia).

28 Some of the interpretations say, of course, that wine is not really wine, but love, etc. However, even reading wine as wine is a sort of subversion already.

29 "Dutch King Willem-Alexander declares the end of the welfare state," available online: http://www. independent.co.uk/news/world/europe/dutch-king-willemalexander-declares-the-end-of-the-welfare-state-8822421.html

30 For an exploration of the important role of *bazaaris* in Iranian society, see Arang Keshavarzian, *Bazaar and State in Iran: The Politics of the Tehran Marketplace*, Cambridge University Press, Cambridge, 2009.

31 "Woman dies of acid attack in Esfahan, former top

Iranian tourist attraction," *Iran News*, October 20, 2014; "Iran Investigates Acid Attacks on Women," Radio Free Europe/Radio Farda, October 19, 2014; "'Bad hijab' link to acid attacks on Iranian women," *al-Arabiyya News*, October 21, 2014; "Iran: Acid attack in Isfahan by organized gangs linked to the mullahs' regime," *Iran News*, October 20, 2014.

3. Libidinal Economy of the October Revolution

1 https://www.marxists.org/archive/marx/works/subject/religion/book-revelations.htm
2 Wilhelm Reich, *The Sexual Revolution: Toward a Self-Governing Character Structure*, Farrar, Straus and Giroux, New York, 1963, p. 185.
3 Wilhelm Reich, "Preface to the Second Edition" (1936), in *The Sexual Revolution*, Farrar, Straus and Giroux, New York, 1986, xxvi–xxvii
4 Dr E. B. Demidovich, *Sud nad polovoi raspuschchennost'iu* (Doloi negramotnost, Moscow and Leningrad, 1927), quoted from Eric Naiman, *Sex in Public: The Incarnation of Early Soviet Ideology*, Princeton University Press, Princeton, NJ, 1997, pp. 132–3.
5 Naiman, *Sex in Public*, pp. 135–6.
6 Naiman, *Sex in Public*, p. 135–6.
7 Roland Barthes, *The Grain of the Voice. Interviews 1962–1980*, Northwestern University Press, Evanston, IL, 2009, p. 302.
8 C. J. Chivers, "A Retrospective Diagnosis Says Lenin Had Syphilis," *New York Times*, June 22, 2004.

9 See Lynn Mally, *Revolutionary Acts: Amateur Theater and the Soviet State, 1917–1938*, Cornell University Press, Ithaca, NY, 2000.

10 Vladimir Mayakovsky, *The Bedbug and Selected Poetry*, Indiana University Press, Bloomington, IN, p. 286.

11 Quoted from Clara Zetkin, *Reminiscences of Lenin*, 1924, available online: https://www.marxists.org/arch ive/zetkin/1924/reminiscences-of-lenin.htm#h07

12 Zetkin, *Reminiscences of Lenin*.

13 Zetkin, *Reminiscences of Lenin*.

14 V. I. Lenin, Letter to Inessa Armand, January 24, 1915, in *Lenin Collected Works*, Progress Publishers, 1976, Moscow, Volume 35, pp. 182–5.

15 Lenin, Letter to Inessa Armand.

16 Quoted according to Roland Barthes, *How To Live Together*, Columbia University Press, New York, 2013, pp. 87–8.

17 *Lenin i Gorkii: Pisma* (Moscow, 1958), pp. 251–2. An English translation is in Maxim Gorky, *Days with Lenin*, Martin Lawrence, New York, 1932, p. 52.

18 R. C. Elwood, *Inessa Armand: Revolutionary and Feminist*, Cambridge University Press, Cambridge, 2002, p. 177.

19 Angelica Balabanoff, interviewed by Bertram D. Wolfe (1953), available online: http://members.optushome. com.au/spainter/Wolfe.html

20 http://www.marxists.org/archive/gould/2003/200309 24b.htm#3

4. The Temptation of Che Guevara

1 Che Guevara, *Guerrilla Warfare*, Rowman & Littlefield Publishers, Lanham, MD, 2002, p. 174.

2 Ernesto Che Guevara, *Che Guevara Reader: Writings on Politics & Revolution*, ed. David Deutschmann, Ocean Press, Melbourne, 2003, pp. 225–6.

3 Libby Brooks, "Che Guevara's Daughter Recalls her Revolutionary Father," *The Guardian*, July 22, 2009.

4 Richard L. Harris, *Che Guevara: A Biography*, Greenwood, Santa Barbara, CA, 2010, p. 164.

5 *Che Guevara Reader*, p. 384.

6 Che Guevara, *The African Dream: The Diaries of the Revolutionary War in the Congo*, Grove Press, New York, 2001, p. 24.

7 Aleida March, *Remembering Che: My Life with Che Guevara*, Ocean Press, Melbourne, 2012, p. 168.

8 March, *Remembering Che*, p. 41.

9 March, *Remembering Che*, p. 50.

10 March, *Remembering Che*, p. 120.

11 Alain Badiou, lecture in Novi Sad, Serbia, January 14, 2015.

12 March, *Remembering Che*, p. 124

13 March, *Remembering Che*, p. 129.

14 Ben Kenigsberg, "Guerrillas in the Mist," *Time Out Chicago*, November 13–19, 2008.

15 Friedrich Nietzsche, "On Reading and Writing," in *Thus Spoke Zarathustra*, Cambridge University Press, Cambridge, 2006, p. 28.

16 March, *Remembering Che*, p. 130.

5. "What Do I Care about Vietnam?"

1 Dieter Kunzelmann, "Notizen zur Gründung revolutionärer Kommunen in den Metropolen," in Albrecht Goeschel (ed.), *Richtlinien und Anschläge, Materialen zur Kritik der repressiven Gesellschaft*, Carl Hanser Verlag, Munich, 1968, p. 100.

2 Kunzelmann, "Notizen zur Gründung revolutionärer Kommunen in den Metropolen."

3 "Wir fordern die Enteignung Axel Springers – Gespräch mit dem Berliner FU-Studenten Rudi Dutschke (SDS)," Der *Spiegel*, July 10, 1967, p. 32, available online: http://www.spiegel.de/spiegel/print/d-46225038.html

4 Uschi Obermeier, *Das wilde Leben*, Hoffman und Campe Verlag, Hamburg, 2000, p. 95.

5 Reinhard Mohr, "Obermaier-Film 'Das Wilde Leben': Boxenluder der Revolution," *Der Spiegel*, January 25, 2007, available online: http://www.spiegel.de/kultur/kino/obermaier-film-das-wilde-leben-boxenluder-der-revolution-a-462051.html

6 Julia Müller, "Miss Kommune und ihr Leben zu acht," in *Twen*, Vol. 11, No. 6, 1969, p. 6.

7 "Wir fordern die Enteignung Axel Springers," p. 32.

8 Holger Meins, "Die Waffe Mensch," in Pieter Bakker Schut (ed.), *Das Info. Briefe von Gefangene aus der RAF aus der Diskussion 1973–1977*, Neuer Malik Verlag, Kiel, 1987, p. 65.

9 Meins, "Die Waffe Mensch," p. 67.

10 Ulrike Meinhof, "Ulrike Meinhof on the Dead Wing," in J. Smith & A. Moncourt (eds), *Red Army Faction,*

Volume 1: Projectiles for the People, PM Press, Oakland, CA, 2011, pp. 271–2.

11 Mark Rudd, *Underground: My Life with SDS and the Weathermen*, William Morrow, New York, 2010, p. 165.

12 Bill Ayers, *Fugitive Days: Memoirs of an Antiwar Activist*, Beacon Press, Boston, MA, 2009, p. 147.

13 Rudd, *Underground*, p. 164.

14 Rudd, *Underground*, p. 31.

Afterplay: the Radicality of Love

1 Jean Baudrillard, *Fatal Strategies*, Semiotext(e), Los Angeles, CA, 1998, pp. 135–6.

2 Daniel Bensaïd, *An Impatient Life: A Memoir*, Verso, London, 2014, p. 98.

3 Simone de Beauvoir, *Letters to Sartre*, Arcade Publishing, New York, 1992, pp. 142–3.

4 https://www.marxists.org/archive/kollonta/1921/theses-morality.htm

5 Alexandra Kollontai, *Selected Writings of Alexandra Kollontai*, Allison & Busby, London, 1977.

6 http://www.un.org/apps/news/story.asp?NewsID=44264&Cr=sexual+violence&Cr1=#.VMPCJUu9bwK

7 See Alexandra Kollontai, *The Autobiography of a Sexually Emancipated Communist Woman*, Prism Key Press, New York, p. 34.

8 I owe this to Sister Teresa Forcades (Catalonia).